Searching For Home

An Autobiography

by

Laurence C. Keene

Copyright

All rights reserved. No part of this book may be reproduced or transmitted in any form or by any means, electronic or mechanical, including photocopying, recording, or by an information storage and retrieval system - except by a reviewer who may quote brief passages in a review to be printed in a magazine or newspaper - without permission in writing from the author.

Printed in the United States of America

Additional copies of this book can be found on Amazon.

Dr. Keene can be found lckeen@aol.com

Cover Design: Robert Arnold
Colorization of Cover: Ernie Merlan

Other Books and Research by Dr. Keene

Moral Attitudes Among Pentecostal and Episcopalians

Abraham-King Elementary School, an experiment in desegregation and multicultural education: a case-study analysis

Heirs of Stone and Campbell on the Pacific Slope; a sociological approach; The Forrest R. Reed Lectures, 1984

Communion Meditations and Prayers

Offering Meditations and Prayers

How Can I? Perplexing spiritual questions and suggestive spiritual answers

Hey God. Do you have a minute? Learning to pray earnestly and honestly

Searching for home. (An autobiography)

Dedicated to:

My wife, Virginia,

who pushed me to write what

I didn't believe I could ever write.

Forward

I had previously felt that unless one was a narcissist most people would not purposely choose to write an autobiography of their own life. I have since learned that a great many autobiographies have come from the promptings of close loved ones <u>or</u> the urgings of followers or devotees of one kind or the other. This autobiography is the result of both of these types of encouragements. My wife, Virginia, had been urging me for years to write down the experiences of my life to share with our children, our grand-children, and our great-grandchildren. "You are the only one who knows the facts and feelings of your life" she would say to me on numerous occasions. "Once you are gone from us there will be no one left who would be around to talk about or tell us fully what you could have told us while you were alive" she would say to me again and again. For decades I would give her one excuse after another as to why I would wait and do it later or why I wasn't sure I would even do it at all. My children and grandchildren began to also echo Virginia's words as well: "Please, Grandpa. We would really like to know more about your very interesting life!" they would say to me from time to time.

Recently, a very disturbing moment was revealed to me on television when I was seeing pictures of little children being forcibly separated from their immigrant parents and being put in terrible cages at many of the border entries of our country. Those images struck me as being profoundly cruel and hurtful. I found myself openly crying in a way I neither immediately understood or could explain. Then, all of a sudden, I began to understand. I began to realize that I was not only crying for the pain these little children were experiencing. I was also crying for the buried pain I had experienced in the early years of my life when I was forcibly separated from my parents as well. I began to realize that I was still experiencing some deep pain within me as well. I started to remember those early childhood years of mine when I and my younger three sisters were taken by the county officials in Seattle, Washington to live in an orphanage for an indeterminate period of time and then later on, to move to two separate foster homes in rural Washington State for three years. I quickly understood the tremendous value of what Virginia had tried for decades to get me to do. I slowly began to feel I needed to write down my biography not just to inform my family of my troubled and challenging past but to put down in writing the story of my life as an important means of my bringing those buried events in my past closer to the surface of my mind in order to bring about the emotional release and, hopeful, the healing I personally needed within me.

This is exactly what writing this short autobiography has done for me. It has brought me a sense of healing I don't think I could have experienced had I not recorded my buried, painful, memories down on paper. I started writing down my earliest half-remembered thoughts which began with me 86 years ago. I included not only those factual incidents I could remember but I also tried to write down, as best I could do, how I felt about those factual moments as well. It has become both a facts book and a feelings book about my life. This was a wise choice on my part. It was the first time I came to realize that those deep and sometimes very disturbing feelings about my past belonged to me just as much as did the factual experiences that had occurred to me in my earlier life. After I had written down on paper the very first few pages of my autobiography, I found myself going to my wife, Virginia, and excitedly began asking her if I could read what I had just written about the first memories I could recall from the earliest years of my young life. We then began to 'cry a river' together as an old popular song once spoke about. Over and over again my creative process would continue with me writing and with Virginia joining me in the reading of my written words. We cried and laughed together through the chapters of my freshly-revealed life until a deep, emotional cleansing slowly began to take place within me. Rivers and rivers of tears, laughter, and shared reflections with Virginia lead to a wonderful sense of healing that is still continuing to this day.

My initial reaction to being encouraged to write my biography was: "I don't have that much I can actually remember that anyone else would want to know about." What I discovered in going through the process of reflection and writing was that each story I could remember led to another forgotten story that would somehow bubble to the surface of my consciousness. It was as if each episode in my memory was a single brick in a long brick fence. As each brick was removed from the fence of my forgotten past, other bricks began to fall out of my imprisoned past until a large part of these forgotten memories began to reappear for me as if they had just occurred a short time ago.

I hope that each person who reads this autobiography will enjoy peeking through the open windows of the life I have provided them to look at. I hope this glance in my direction will not only give everyone a clearer vision of where I have come from in my life's journey and what I have experienced and learned along the way, but I hope people will also gain a sense of what I felt inside me while going from here to there along that way. I suppose no one can ever include everything about one's own life in their writing about it, for there will surely be some parts of one's life that will be permanently forgotten or purposely deemed totally unimportant to share with others. However, I hope there is enough contained in this account of my life to give others some appreciation of the who, the what, the where, and the why of the first-born child of my teen-age parents, LeRoy and Agnes Keene. I have learned that some of what is included in this autobiography reveals my continuing search for a home that was once taken away from me when I was a little child. Have I found this lost home of mine completely yet? Yes, in most ways I have. I have found a sense of 'home' in the 66-year marriage to my wonderful wife, Virginia, and in the close and rewarding connections I have forged and enjoyed with our five children and their five spouses, our 22 grandchildren and their spouses as well and, of course, also in the lives of our six young great-grandchildren. I have also felt wonderfully at home and rewarded in my 67 years as a Christian minister and in my 42 years as a university professor of sociology and anthropology. People have often referred to me in the past as being a home-body. I suppose I am. I have searched and discovered so much of what I had previously lost as a child when I was taken from the home my parents had first provided for me. But to be truthful, some of those old feelings of abandonment that settled within my soul when I was taken away from that earliest home are still, in some very small ways, being felt within me today. I have a deep and curious nature that continues to search for the 'more' that is implied in the idea of a 'home'. I have learned that once a glass of refreshing life-giving water has been filled to its very brim that it can still continue to bless and refresh others by what can be retrieved from its overflow. That expanded sense of the 'more' which I am continuing to find in my searching for it, is continuing to bless me even in this present moment and I hope that the reader of this written work will also be blessed and refreshed from the overflow because of this continuing search of mine.

Laurence C. Keene, Summer, 2023

Table of Contents

Being very young in my Washington State home. 1

My time of painful separation from home. 25

That step toward the home that education provided me. 43

Finding my religious home. 57

Leaving my borrowed home and re-entering my real one. 63

Difficult talks in my home about the Big War. 83

Games and other rituals in my home. 97

The stern mother that lived with me in my home. 107

That special bond with my father in my home. 123

My search for home through secondary education 145

College life, a new kind of home for me. 181

Finding my home in the ministry 199

My new Indiana home. 229

My new California home. 249

Learning to wear two hats in my growing home. 265

My two new Valley homes. 281

My final steps toward receiving my doctorate 291

Building our unique valley church 309

Finally, finding my ultimate home and then some. 329

1

Being very young in my Washington State home.

I held up five fingers one day when someone asked me the question: "How old are you, Larry?" I thought to myself: "Has it been one year already since I held up four fingers when someone asked me the same question?" I noticed that none of my little friends ever asked me that question. Only the tall people seemed to do that.

"Where do you live?" was another question the tall people used to ask me a lot. I couldn't answer questions like that with my fingers so I had to learn to memorize the correct answers to these kind of questions. "Seattle!" was the answer I was quickly able to give them. There were several things I could also tell the tall people about Seattle if they really wanted to know, which most of them did not. "Seattle has lots of hills" I could also quickly say to them or that "Seattle has lots of rain" was another piece of information I had memorized and could pass on to the tall people. And of most importance to me (and I think to all the other little children my age) was the fact that Seattle also had lots of tar in the cracks of their concrete streets. In the summer the warm sun would heat up the broken sections of concrete in the streets that were held together by generous applications of tar. This was the tar that would get soft and gooey in the summer heat. This was perfect for the prying five-year-old-fingers of little boys and girls like me. Our working-class family could not afford chewing gum for their four children but that didn't bother us little ones one bit. We had a whole street full of chewing gum right in front of our white, run-down, little apartment where we lived. We children felt blissfully fortunate to have lived in the great place we did. Our teeth and mouth and fingers and clothes were quickly blackened by all that played-in and consumed tar. No one hardly noticed the blackness on our bodies and clothing because of the huge and contented smiles on the faces of my three younger sisters and me and our little friends who were similarly afflicted with great smiles. That is, no one noticed all the tar except my mother!

My mother was married at 15 years of age and gave birth to all four of us children by the time she was 19 years old. She did a lot of yelling at us children. It seemed to me at the time that she had very little patience with people, especially with small ones. Even at five years of age I came to understand that perhaps she might have had more patience if she had given birth to less children less quickly. While my mother was sometimes very unhappy with the way we children were playing on those Seattle streets in 1942, nothing could dim the happiness we, ourselves, felt by playing there. The clear picture that remains in my mind to this very day is not just the warm concrete and gooey black tar the city streets provided us to enjoy but also the wonderful image in my mind of at least ten other little children huddled close together on the curb of that Seattle street as well. We didn't quite understand what the word 'friend' meant but that is exactly what we were. We were friends. It was the friendship, not just the tar that I remember enjoying so much in those early days. Ten little friends with ten very black faces in filthy tar-stained clothing smiling from ear to ear. That is what I still remember. That was the very embodiment of the kind of happiness I have learned to this day that every successful parent wants their little children to experience in life.

The warm, tar-filled streets were my most-cherished playground in Seattle in 1942. My red tricycle, however, was my most-cherished possession on that playground. I don't know how or where that tricycle came from. From the looks of the broken-down condition of that tricycle it was probably left somewhere in some alley when the former occupants of our apartment decided to move away. This sorry-looking tricycle was not an item that people would put into a moving truck to save for their next place of residence. But to me, that red tricycle became a treasure I came to greatly cherish. That tricycle was the ugly duckling of all the tricycles in our neighborhood. The little seat on my 'bike' (as I called it) was rusted at a permanent angle of about five or six degrees off center to the right. The handle bar was also rusted in a permanently locked position in the opposite direction to the same degree. So, to successfully ride my bike the bottom part of my body was pointed in one direction and the top part of my body was always pointed in another. It was almost impossible to ride my bike in a straight line. I didn't have to worry very much, however, because I was never able to go very fast in this cherished treasure of mine. Big chunks of rubber were missing on the front hard-rubber tire of my bike causing me to run part of the time on the rubber part of my rim while running the rest of the time on the metal part of the rim itself. There was no way I could build up much speed in this red beauty. Did I say red? Someone had painted this ugly duckling tricycle the color red with a paintbrush that must have been missing half of its bristles. There were no spray cans of paint in those days. My description of the 'ugly duckling' bike does not just come from the out-of-line seat and crooked handlebars and a front tire that looked like the missing teeth of a small child. A big part of the ugliness of my little bike came from the very crude paint job itself. But, as my bike may have appeared ugly to some people, this red tricycle seemed like a work of art to me. I especially liked the plastic handle-bar grip on the right side of my handle-bar. It had multi-colored plastic tassels flowing from inside the plastic grip which hung down about six inches on the right side of my bike. It never dawned on me that I should have had another matching plastic grip and set of tassels on the left side of the handle-bar, which it did not have. Most of my waking hours outside my apartment were spent on the street with the gooey tar and on my bike exploring that neighborhood. Moving along with the total misalignment of my body, I pedaled my 'beautiful' bike down those Seattle streets and alleys with no awareness at all of how funny I must have looked to others while I was bumping along with my front wheel missing at least one-half of its rubber on its rusty rim. To those curious onlookers I was probably just a little boy blissfully moving along into his new and exciting world of exploration all on his own. It was, for sure, a carefree, tricycle-world. My contented face showed just how happy this little boy truly was in that new world of his own making!

At five years of age I knew I wasn't very big but I quickly learned from my mother that I was now the big brother in the family. What that meant to me was that I had three younger sisters and that I had been delegated with a very important job as far as these younger girls were concerned. I learned that it was my job to look after them at all times. Those were the very broad but important instructions handed down by my mother to me whose diminished patience and energy had expected me to take some of the weight off her shoulders in the child-care department. I was specifically instructed to: keep sharp objects from being used by the girls; to keep small objects from entering their mouths; to keep the girls from entering any street unattended; and, of course, to not allow the girls to climb up on high places from which they could fall and get hurt. Additional clarification of her concerns for the girls were added to my duty-list on a fairly regular basis. Being a big brother was a big deal to my mother. I didn't really like the title nor the job. For me, it simply meant more time away from my bike and my exciting neighborhood explorations.

It quickly became apparent to me that I was not a very good big brother because my little sisters managed to create a whole lot of trouble in our little apartment. My three sisters were very imaginative in their misdeeds. My mother always put her hair up at night in pin-curlers. When she was finished her entire head was covered with little circles of hair neatly pinned down by hairpins to dry overnight. My three-year old sister, Roberta, had just learned how to make a pair of scissors work successfully in her little hands. My mother was a very sound sleeper and she had no idea that at the very moment she was taking an afternoon nap that little Roberta was practicing her newly-learned skill of using those scissors. While I was watching the other two children, Roberta began removing those neatly pinned-down curls of hair from my mother's head with the scissors she had just learned to, quite proudly, operate. One-half of all those curls were liberated from my mother's head before my mother finally woke up. "Look at all the pretty curls I found, Mommy!" were the only words Roberta had to say to her. My mother had a lot of angry words to say to ME! Sharp instruments in the hands of the little girls were on the big-brother list of things I was responsible for them not having. I was busted by my mother big time! What my mother lacked in patience she more than made up for with her anger. I felt the full impact of her wrath that afternoon. In that moment I so wished I had been born in 1939 rather than in 1937. Then, my younger sister Marlene could have been the big brother, not me!

Both of my parents came from very large families. Dad was one of twelve children. Mother came from a family of ten children. There were nine girls and one boy in mother's family. Ralph, the one boy in the family, ended up having ten mothers in the family and because of that became very spoiled and self-centered. I remember as a small child asking my mother that when he came for a visit to our house why he always talked about himself so much and how often he told us children how good he was at doing this or that kind of thing or how smart he was at certain subjects. She explained to me that it was because he was the only boy in the family and that he was spoiled. I didn't understand what the word 'spoiled' meant but I told mother that I was worried that I would someday become spoiled too because I was the only boy with three little sisters. My mother assured me that she didn't think that would ever happen to me but my sisters insisted, in later life, that it surely already had happened to me!

My parents moved away from all of their siblings shortly after they got married. At different times they confided in us children, when we were old enough to understand, that many of their brothers and sisters would not be a good influence for us little children. Several of their siblings had been in prison on multiple occasions. Several had great difficulty holding down a job for any lengthy period of time and were generally lazy and unmotivated people. My parents felt that the farther away they could move from such negative influences would be a good thing for us children. So, for the most part, any association through the years with our cousins and other relatives were short-lived moments usually centered around some particular holiday event. This forced separation from our two ancestral families meant that we did not get to know our grandparents and our other relatives very well. Both of my grandfathers had already passed away by the time we children were born so I do not have any recollection of my grandfathers at all. I do remember that my father's mother was very short. She was probably a couple inches short of being five feet tall. She was very round in her shape and put her hair up in a round bun at the top of her head. But, the one thing I remember the most about my father's mother is that she had several long whiskers on her chin that tickled me whenever she bent over to kiss me. She was a sweet and friendly lady but I have to admit I had a difficult time getting past her whiskers. Once when we came to her house she had an object all wrapped up in wax paper that looked like a brick. It was quite heavy and smelled like alcohol when it was unwrapped. I was told it was a fruit-cake. I was so excited about this because I really liked most fruit and I certainly liked cake. However, when I took a big bite of Grandma's Keene's work of culinary art the alcohol hit my tongue and there was an immediate involuntary rejection of all of the contents in my mouth. The food in my mouth went flying across the room and I screamed for some water to cool the burning in my mouth and throat. This was clearly not a cake for children and that fruit tasted like no other fruit I had ever tasted before. I have since learned that fruit-cake concoctions are an acquired taste that few people develop. It is, I believe, on the endangered list today of favored food items in America. I really tried to create a warm place in my heart for my Grandma Keene but her chin-whiskers and her fruit-cake made that desire a real challenge for me. It was probably a good thing for me that

Grandma Keene lived quite a distance from us so our contacts with each other were infrequent. I loved her hugs and cheerful demeanor. Her chin-whiskers and fruit-cake, not so much!

Grandma Anderson was a little different. My mother's mother did not live very close to our house either so our visits together were infrequent through the years but were very joyful moments when they did occur. Her cute little chin had no prickly whiskers nor did she make fruit-cake with alcohol in it. There was never any alcohol at all in her home as she was a Christian of a non-alcoholic kind. She was the grandma who taught us Bible songs that were specially designed for children to sing. She was a member of the Salvation Army Church. She often joined a small musical band of 'Soldiers for Christ' who would play, sing, and preach on the street corners of Tacoma, Washington. For years our grandma was one of those street-corner preachers who would try to reach out and speak to the hearts of those passing by to save them from their lives of sin and desperation. She had a wonderful heart and we grandchildren loved her for it. One of the most painful emotional experiences in my life involved my grandmother Anderson several years later in my life. My grandmother lived on a very small pension each month. Penny-pinching was the guiding principle of her monthly existence. When I graduated much later from high-school she purchased a leather-bound Schofield Bible for my graduation gift. It was no ordinary Schofield Bible. It was the best and most expensive Bible the Schofield Company made. It cost her the equivalent of her entire monthly pension check to purchase. I delayed and delayed in finding the right moment to write her a thank-you note for her gift to me until my dear grandmother did not delay in finding the right moment to die! It was one of the most humiliating and painful moments of my life. It was also one of the great lessons I have ever learned. I learned that if a person doesn't express his or her gratitude in a timely manner then that person may not ever get the opportunity to do so, which is what happened to me. When our spoken gratitude for another person's goodness to us is delayed it might as well not come at all because the other person may correctly assume that our gratitude is not sufficiently sincere when it does come. I remember standing at the side of my grandmother's casket at her funeral feeling not just the pain of her loss in my life but the stinging humiliation of my own tardy sense of gratitude I failed to show her at an appropriate time in my life!

My family was very poor, as my parents explained to me much later when I could understand such things. However, I did not think that being poor was a particularly bad thing in those days. We were like everyone else that lived near us. We were all poor. That seemed to make it reasonably okay. We were all in this poverty thing together. My parents were very creative in the ways they distracted us from the dreariness of living in our very poor neighborhood. Each year, when the rainy weather of Washington State subsided long enough to give us a few weeks of absolutely beautiful sunny days, they would take us away for what they informed us would be a vacation. "What's a vacation?" I would ask our father. He said to me: "A vacation is a time when we can get away from our home and go to another place and have the most wonderful time of our life. A vacation is a fun time for both children and adults alike." As you can imagine we could hardly wait for the vacation times to come. The best vacation we ever had, the entire family all agreed, was when we packed up our old 1936 Studebaker sedan with camping gear, food, and all six of us. We headed west along the Columbia River to the Pacific Ocean. We could camp on the ocean beach for free and we could also build a big fire next to our tent. We roasted wieners and put cans of pork 'n beans in the hot coals of the big bon-fire for dinner. We had marshmallows for dessert which we roasted by using old clothes hangers which we had straightened out and hung over the fire until the marshmallow turned black. Later in the evening all six of us crawled inside our old army-issue sleeping bags inside our big army-issue tent that my dad had purchased at the Army-surplus store. Listening to the sound of the waves pounding on the beach made it feel as if we were spending the night at the very best hotel in the world. We all felt that there could not have been a better night's lodging anywhere. When the rain fell at night (as it always did on the beach at night) its hypnotizing sound pounding on the outside of the tent quickly put all of us to sleep. I remember to this very day how quieting to the soul was the rhythmic sound of rain pelting on the outside skin of our tent especially when it was combined with the never-ending pulsating sounds of the waves pounding on the beach, over and over and over again. It is now, as it was then years ago to me, heaven's medicine for a good night's sleep. In the morning it was corn-flake cereal for breakfast and then we were all given little buckets and little shovels to hunt for lunch. "What's for lunch?" I asked dad. "Clams." he said back to me. "We are having clams for lunch?" I said. "I have never had clams before, Dad." I said excitedly. "You are going to have clams today, Larry!" Dad said. So, after a few instructive words from Dad about hunting for clams, we all went running down the beach armed with buckets, shovels, and a whole lot of enthusiasm to capture those illusive clam creatures. And, we found them. They were hiding in the sand just as Dad said they would be and after several trial and error efforts by us little ones, all of our buckets were filled with clams and we all happily and hurriedly made our way back to our tent where mother was standing to see our brimming buckets filled with our gray clam shells. The big fire was nearby and we noticed that the big galvanized wash tub we often bathed in at home was half-filled with hot boiling water over the fire. "We have to go down to the ocean now and wash the clams." Dad said to us kids, so we all loudly screamed as we raced each other to the ocean to give the clams a good bath. Back at the tent, dad said to us all: "Now take your buckets with the clean clams and pour them, shells and all, into the boiling water and watch carefully to the change that happens to them." Before long all the clams began to open up and we could see those beautiful soft clam creatures revealed inside. "They are very delicious." Dad said to us children. "You can scoop the clams out of their shells with a fork and put some salt and pepper on them, or you can dip them into some sauce your mother has prepared, or you can just put the soft clam directly into your mouth without anything on it at all." The three girls opted for the sauce choice, consuming much more sauce than clams as I remember. I watched Dad pry open his clam shell with his fork and he put the little clam directly into his mouth. I decided that that was the way I would do it too.

Yummy! I was hooked! No sauce, no pepper, and no salt for me that day. Just that soft and juicy morsel that I had rescued from its precious hiding place at the edge of the Pacific Ocean!

2

My time of painful separation from home.

The Second World War with Germany and Japan created many casualties at home in America as well as it did overseas. Our little family was one of those war-time casualties. The rising war-fever among the young men in our country to volunteer in joining the fighting of these two enemies was reaching its peak in the city of Seattle in 1942. My father, even though he would be leaving four little children at home, was one of those young men who stepped forward to stand in this line of volunteers for warfare. I quickly learned a new word in 1942. It was the word 'war.' Several attempts were made by the tall people to explain to me what that word meant but what it meant to me was simply this:

my father was now gone from me. He was gone from all of us in the family of course, but most of all I could not help but feel he was gone from me most of all! It was explained to me that other people needed my daddy more than I needed him right now and that he would come back to me someday. That made no sense to me. "How could anyone need him more than I did?" I thought to myself. I began counting on my fingers the weeks that had passed since he left our little apartment. I could count quite high at five years of age so I kept counting until I had no more fingers left to count the time with. Somehow, that made me even more sad. Not only could I not get my head around all this war talk, I couldn't even get my fingers around it either!

A very strange thing happened shortly after my daddy left our house for the war. It disturbed me greatly and I could not understand it at all.

Another man began sleeping with my mother in the same bed Daddy had been sleeping in. When I asked my mother who this man was she said to me: "Why, he is your uncle Jules." I did not understand why uncle Jules was sleeping where daddy had been sleeping. All I knew was that I quickly didn't like my uncle Jules. I don't know why I felt that way. I just knew I didn't like Uncle Jules at all!

It was not long before another personal war-time casualty descended upon our little home. Mother was crying and crying and several people I had never met before were helping her pack some clothing for my three little sisters and me. "You will be going somewhere with these nice people and I will come and get you real soon," were the words my mother spoke to me. So first, my father was gone from our home and now my sisters and I would be gone from it as well. And before I could hardly take a breath, we were gone from that little apartment where I had been the big brother. Gone, also, from the warm, gooey tar. Gone from my little friends. Gone from my crying mother and gone from my beautiful red bike. Within what seemed to me to be a very long time riding in a strange car we had never ridden in before, my sisters and I finally arrived at the place where these tall people were taking us. It was a very large building we had never seen before. One of these people in the car that I did not know called that building an 'orphanage' but I had never heard that word before so I did not have any idea what that word meant. All I remembered from that moment on was that when we entered this very large building my sisters were taken in one direction inside the building and I was guided in another. For the very first time in our lives we four children were being separated from each other. I was gone from my father. Gone from my mother. And, now, I was gone from my sisters as well. "Who would be their big brother if I was not with them?" I thought to myself.

I was taken to the biggest room I had ever seen in my life. I found out much later that there were over 200 beds in that big room. They called those beds: 'cots.' I had never heard that word before. I was certainly learning a lot of new words that day. "This will be where you will sleep at night," the person who taught me the word 'orphanage' said to me. Later in the day all the boys in that big room were led outside to play on a giant playground. I noticed a high chain-link fence that divided the playground in half. I went over to the fence and looked through it and saw as many little girls on the other side of the fence as there were little boys on my side of the fence.

And there, not too far from me, were my three sisters . . . crying. I yelled as loud as I could the name of my oldest sister, Marlene. She lifted her head in my direction and then she came running with her other two little blonde-haired sisters running after her. We poked our fingers through the chained-link fence and intertwined them together as if we would never ever let go of them. Four of us forlorn little ones crying in unison! We continued to meet there each day at playtime. We didn't need to play. We needed to touch and touch and touch each other's fingers! And so, touch and touch we did for the many months we were at the orphanage. We didn't have the appropriate words for that occasion but we did have the appropriate feelings. That touch did for us what the missing words could never do. I cannot actually say how long my sisters and I were at that orphanage. It seemed like years to me but it was probably only months. In my mind, however, it will always seem like years to me because that is exactly the way it felt to that little five-year old boy. I will never forget the sights, sounds, and odors of that place. Every time I enter a public bathroom today and smell an over-chlorinated room I think of that orphanage. Every time I see a little child separated and standing all by himself or herself in a crowded space filled with other little children, I think of that orphanage. Every time I see a piece of toast that is buttered only in the center and not buttered along its edges or into its four corners, I think of that orphanage. Every time I see a chain-link fence with little children touching each other's fingers through the openings in the two sides of that fence, I think of that orphanage. That orphanage is not ever very far from me even to this very day. That orphanage-experience has visited me quite often in the past 80-plus years!

As I just said, for many years I did not understand why my mother sent us children away so soon after our father had gone away to the war. "Did she not want us anymore?" I once thought to myself. "Was it something we had done to upset her?" was a dark thought I nursed for a while. When I was much older I thought that perhaps she simply could not afford to care for us any longer. Many years later I finally learned that none of these circumstances were true at all. I learned from some of my relatives that with all the pressures of that wartime period and the fact that my mother's health was never very good in the first place, that my mother had experienced a severe mental and physical breakdown and the health authorities in the county stepped in to care for the entire family in the best way they knew how to do at the time.

After some long period of time in the orphanage we were moved from the orphanage to two separate foster homes. My two middle sisters, Marlene and Roberta, were sent to a home on Vashon Island in the midst of the Puget Sound in Washington state. Judy, the youngest of my sisters, and I were sent to Herb and Martha Swain's 40-acre farm near the little town of Enumclaw, Washington. Judy and I were very fortunate in this foster-home arrangement because the Swain household was a home where considerable love was shown toward everyone . . . especially toward little Judy. The Swains already had two older boys and I had the feeling they took me just so they could get a cute little blonde girl in the deal. Marlene and Roberta have described to me that their foster-home experience was one of bitterness and unhappiness. Separation from one's original birth home is enough pain for any child to carry with them through life but to add to that the additional climate of bitterness and unhappiness my other two sisters endured on a daily basis is more than I can even begin to fully imagine. My sisters never talked very much about their experiences away from their family home and I think I can understand why. Painful reveries, I have discovered in life, are never entered into willingly or frequently. Who would ever want to re-visit such a terribly painful experience again by talking about it? So, my sisters never did.

Forty acres of farmland was not like being in Seattle with a red tricycle but it became a new and challenging experience for a six-year old boy who had just had a birthday since he came to the farm. The Swains had a great big red barn on the farm and lots and lots of cows, horses, pigs, and chickens on it too. It quickly became my job to collect the eggs the chickens laid each day and to bring them into the house. I also got to help feed the pigs but since the pigs were much bigger than I was I was not allowed to go into their pig-pen without an adult to watch over me. The two older brothers, Leonard and Ronald, who were ten and twelve years of age, qualified as adults so they could go into the pig pen with me. The older brothers loved lording it over me in the pig-pen as they had no one else to lord it over in life until I came along. I was not allowed to get even by lording it over my little sister, Judy, since Mr. and Mrs. Swain made it very clear to me that she was their little 'princess.' Even though I was the oldest of the newcomers to the farm it was made clear to me that my rank was the lowest overall.

That lowly rank continued that way for the three years we were there on the farm.

The horses did the heaviest and hardest work on the farm. They pulled the wagons, the plows, the harvest rake used to gather the hay in the fields, and the many other large farm tools Mr. Swain used in cultivating and preparing the fields for harvest time. These magnificent horses would also carry (in a large wagon) the many tree stumps to the dump that were blown out of the ground with dynamite by Mr. Swain. He would clear large areas of forest land with this dynamite so he could expand the amount of land that was available for growing the crops they would need for food for the many animals they had. In 1942, most of the farming in our country was done with animals as the machinery that was being produced in our country was mostly being manufactured for the war effort. The Swains partially supported themselves by selling the milk they milked from their cows. All this milking was done by hand. No machines of any kind were used on their farm. To get all this milking done meant getting up while it was very dark in the morning. Mr. Swain, Leonard the twelve year-old son, and Ronald the ten year-old son, did all the milking. I tried to squeeze some milk out of the cows' teats but I was not strong enough to get any fluid to come out of the cows. It was made quite clear to me by Mr. Swain that I was stuck with the egg job for a while. When I complained that I wanted a more grown-up kind of job I was given a promotion. I was handed a square-bladed shovel and taken to the manure trough at the foot of where the cows stood in the barn and I was told to begin shoveling the manure the cows left in the trough into the wheel-barrow Mr. Swain had given me. I was to take this stinky collection of manure outside the barn and put my collection on to a large pile of manure that had been placed there. It was explained to me by Mr. Swain that all this stinky manure from the cows and horses would be spread throughout the farm on the vegetables and various grains that were growing there so it could be used to help grow the feed that was given to the animals to eat. I didn't like this new promotion Mr. Swain had given me! I should have kept my mouth shut and been content with collecting eggs! This new promotion was a dirty, messy, and did I say stinky, job? I could hardly wait until my hands got stronger so I could be promoted to squeezing some of that precious white juice from those teats!

I did not know what the word 'melancholy' meant in those early days on the farm, but I knew how it felt. I was very sad much of the time.

Little Judy, my sister, was too young to feel that deep feeling of loneliness I felt in my heart for my parents. The two older boys, Leonard and Ronald, were in a world all their own and were content with staying there. They had no room for me in that world of theirs. Almost every evening I would go outside in the darkness and look up at the stars in the sky and recite this poem I had learned from someone earlier in my life:

> *Star light, star bright,*
>
> *first star I see tonight,*
>
> *I wish I may, I wish I might*
>
> *have the wish I wish tonight.*

I would then say out loud the same wish I continued to make each night for the next three years: "Please send my daddy home to me real soon so we could be a family again."

My melancholy time was spent mostly alone in the barn. I carved out a play-corner in the wood-shed that I claimed for my own. I found an old steering wheel discarded from a car that was no longer running. I nailed that wheel to the wall in my private corner and pretended I was a race-car driver. It became the substitute for my gorgeous red bike I once used to explore my Seattle neighborhood. There were no human sounds at all coming from that great big wood-shed . . . except mine. They were the sounds of an automobile racing at high speed up and down imaginary streets and around imaginary corners. They were the sounds of screeching brakes being applied again and again to avoid hitting dangerous objects in the road. Loud horns were being honked from that make-believe automobile to warn pedestrians to quickly move out of my way. One could not imagine that such a quiet little boy could create such tremendous loudness all on his own. That steering wheel was being turned at such breakneck speed that one would think that it would either spin off the wall entirely or that it would bore a hole in the wall that was holding it in place. But, when I came back to visit that wood-shed and that imaginary play-corner of mine 50 years later, that venerable steering wheel was still situated firmly in place just waiting for the next six year-old child to come along and take it for a ride down the street!

3

That step toward the home that education provided me.

I didn't know what the word 'school' meant but I was quickly about to learn. The Swains told me that very soon I had to go to school. School, they explained to me, was a place I had to go to learn things. They told me that first I had to learn how to read words that were written on paper. I told them I already knew how to do that. I told them that my father had already been reading to me for a couple of years and that I could read many words from the cartoon pages in the daily newspaper. The Swains were very surprised to learn that fact about me since none of the children my age knew how to read anything yet in their little rural town. They explained that I had to go to school anyway because there were probably some new and different words that I didn't yet know how to read and that I could learn these words at the new school. The school I was about to go to was a very unusual one by today's standards. It had only one room to it. Located inside my new school were six rows of chairs -- one row for each of the six grades in the school. There was no kindergarten class in this one-room school house I was about to enter. On my first day at school I met Mrs. Fant, the teacher. Mrs. Fant taught all six grades in the school. She taught the first grade for a few minutes and then moved to the second row and taught the second-graders, and so on through the entire assembled group of young scholars. Becoming a teacher myself in my later life, I couldn't imagine how Mrs. Fant was able to do what she did. It was utterly amazing how she managed covering so many subjects and to teach so many different-aged children day after day and year after year. I look back on what she accomplished in that little room and I now can clearly see what a herculean effort it was for her to accomplish what she did. And, what seems more incredible to me as I now reflect upon it, she never ever seemed ruffled at all in doing what she did for such a very long period of time.

On that first day of class we were all given a little book entitled: **Dick and Jane**. Placed on a tripod in front of us was a large, three-by-three foot replica of the little book we all held in our hands. Mrs. Fant opened her large book on the tripod and said to her class of seven first-grade students: "Is there anyone here that can read any of these words?" No one raised their hands but I knew I couldn't just sit there without letting everyone know that I could read those words. As

I just mentioned, my father had read the comics from the newspaper to me each day since I was four years old. I was six when I entered Mrs. Fant's class so by this time I had quite a reading vocabulary of words I could recognize. So, when Mrs. Fant challenged the class to identify some words in the little book, I raised my hand. Mrs. Fant did not say a word to the class but, rather, she just sat there waiting for me to put my hand down. I thought to myself that perhaps she didn't see my hand because I wasn't waving it around hard enough to get her attention so I began waving my arm around with considerable force. "Are you sure you can read this book, Larry?" she finally said to me. "I <u>know</u> I can!" I said with the same energy in my voice that I had shown by raising my waving arm. "Well, go ahead and try." Mrs. Fant said to me. So, I read about Dick and Jane running and kicking the ball and how they could jump and jump and jump. It was quite an exciting introduction to the world of learning for me in that little one-room school-house that day. Needless to say the class was quite impressed and so was Mrs. Fant. I fell in love with education and learning on my very first day at school. Two weeks later Mrs. Fant took me aside and whispered in my ear that she was skipping me forward to the second row. That meant, she explained to me, that she was skipping me forward to the second grade. "I cannot teach you anything you don't already know in the first row." she said to me. "You will have to move to the second row to learn some new information you don't know yet." she confided in me. I was so happy and excited! I didn't know education and learning could be so much fun. One of the ways Mrs. Fant could so successfully teach six classes each day was to have the students help her in doing some of the teaching themselves. When she was instructing one row of students each of the other rows of students in a higher class (except the first graders) would help the younger students next to them with some of their lessons. For instance, the fifth graders would tutor the fourth graders and the third graders would tutor the second graders and so on. This gave everyone extra help from an older child while Mrs. Fant could give extra help to the sixth-grade row because they did not have any older children from which they could be helped. In 1943 when I was in that one-room schoolhouse, that very practice Mrs. Fant employed at that time has since been shown to be pretty enlightened educational philosophy. That very same teaching approach she employed then is sometimes used today in many progressive school programs around the country.

When each school day was over in the afternoon I walked home all alone to the Swain's house. It was a one-mile walk down a gravel road to their farm. That meant going to school was a two-mile trek for me each day. One mile going and one mile returning back home. I always had a pocket filled with good-sized rocks because often when I would be going home a large coyote would venture out onto that road and would take a long, menacing look in my direction. Mr. Swain told me to throw a rock or two and it would run away from me. I had to do that several times so, in time, I got more and more brave in making that solitary walk home. When I think back on those moments today I find myself asking whether I would have allowed my first-grade child to walk down a road where coyotes might be walking along with him or her. I certainly don't think I would do such a thing at all. Ignorance is certainly bliss sometimes, I suppose.

I will never forget the day Mrs. Fant, my wonderful teacher, whispered in my ear for the second time that she was planning on skipping me once again to a higher grade in school. I was in the third grade when this happened and she said to me that she was planning on skipping me from the third grade to the fourth grade. I was only seven years old at the time. What joy I felt when she said that! Now I could sit in the fourth row with the very big children who were two years older than me at the time. I had to whisper back to her, however, that I had just been told by Mr. and Mrs. Swain that I would be going home very soon to my real mother and father's house and that I wouldn't be here at this school much longer. She explained to me that, unfortunately, there probably would not be enough time for her to get all the proper paperwork completed in time to make it possible for me to move to the fourth grade so quickly. This sad news was balanced by the fact, as she explained to me, that perhaps it was to my advantage that I not skip to another higher grade so soon because it would not be an easy adjustment in my future schooling for me to always be two years younger than all of my fellow classmates. I came to understand and appreciate her wisdom all the more as the years passed by. But the thought of learning new and exciting lessons that the other children my age were not privileged to learn was a thrilling thought to me. I knew I could have done it. I knew that I could have handled the more demanding learning required of the fourth-grade students. I knew it as sure as I knew the words in the **Dick and Jane** reading book.

Fifty years later I took my wife and children back to Washington State to see that one-room school-house and to meet Mrs. Fant. I found out that the one-room school-house was still there but that it had been converted into a rural fire station. None of the fire personnel knew of the glorious history that had taken place within those four walls of the very building they now occupied on a daily basis. Several years after this return visit to see Mrs. Fant my daughter, Nancy, took her family on a trip from California to Washington State to also visit my one-room school house as well and to visit with the fire-personnel who still occupied that building. It was quite fun for Nancy to explain to these folk all the many details about the little school as I had experienced them so many years earlier. They were all thrilled to learn of these details that had never been so fully relayed to them before.

When Virginia, I, and the children returned later to the State of Washington to see the old one-room schoolhouse, we inquired in the neighborhood whether Mr. and Mrs. Fant were still alive and we were told that they both were in their eighties and that they were, indeed, very much alive. I drove with my family to their country residence and found Mr. Fant outside doing some light chores in the yard. We all got out of the car and walked up to him and I said to him: "Mr. Fant, I was a former student of your wife's in the early 1940's and I wanted to come back to thank her, personally, for what she did for me as a student and to thank her for the wonderful influence she had made to my life. He said to me: "I will ask her to come out and talk to you but please don't tell her who you are. Give her a little clue as to your identity and see if she can guess your name." She came out of the house in her bathrobe and slippers and I said to her: "Mrs. Fant, I was a student of yours in 1942 when your niece, Linda, was also in your first-grade class. When you asked the students on the first day of class whether any one of us could read the words in the big **Dick and Jane** reading book, which you had propped up on a tripod in front of the first-graders, I said to you that I could read those words. Then I proceeded with your encouragement to read the book until you finally stopped me." Mrs. Fant looked at me with a big smile on her face and she said in a strong voice that all of us could hear: "Why, you are Larry Keene!" We both hugged each other and I looked around and everyone was crying, including Mrs. Fant and me. I said to her: "Do you have any idea what profession I went into in my adult life?" She said to me: "Why of course I do. You became a teacher." I explained to her that I had, indeed, been a professor of sociology and anthropology at Pepperdine University in California for forty years. She was not surprised at all. A couple of weeks later, after we had all returned home to California, I heard that Mrs. Fant had passed away. How fortunate my family and I felt in our hearts to have made that long trip to my early home in Washington State to see that steering-wheel of mine in Mr. and Mrs. Swain's big red shed and to see my dear and beloved teacher, Mrs. Fant, as well.

4

Finding my religious home.

Our childhood memories of past events, I have found out, do not always reflect accurately what actually took place in those long-ago years we try to remember. I had always thought that it was Mr. and Mrs. Swain's devotion to God and the church that led to my life-long love and devotion for things religious or spiritual. On our trip to Washington State to see Mrs. Fant, Virginia and I also spent some time visiting Mrs. Swain, my foster parent for three years when I was there. We were told, sadly, that Mr. Swain had passed away a number of years earlier. Virginia thanked Mrs. Swain for instilling in me and Judy a love for the religious or spiritual life by taking us to Sunday school and church while we were living with them. She explained to Mrs. Swain that had Larry not been involved in the life of the church that she might not have ever met and married him nor would we have had all the wonderful children and grandchildren and great-grandchildren we now enjoyed so much. Mrs. Swain told Virginia that things didn't happen that way at all. She explained to Virginia that the way it actually occurred was the very opposite of that. Early in the placement of us two little foster children in her home, she explained to Virginia, little Judy and Larry were sitting in a corner of her house singing a Sunday school song with the words that said: "Jesus loves me this I know, for the Bible tells me so." Mrs. Swain told her husband, Herb, that: "these children must have had some previous church experience and if this was so then we as foster-parents should make an effort to get these children enrolled in a Sunday school somewhere." Martha Swain told Virginia that their family had never gone to church anywhere before but she felt the need to look after our spiritual development as children. What Mrs. Swain did not know was that we children had never ever gone to church either at that point but that we had a grandmother who was active in the Salvation Army movement. Every time our grandmother came to our house (which was not very often) she would teach us these little religious songs that were specially designed for children. Apparently, we somehow remembered several of these songs and when we went to our new foster home we sang them to each other to bring us the comfort we needed in those melancholy early moments in the Swain household. How powerful this revealing moment was to Virginia and me when we heard Mrs. Swain's words that day! Because Mr. and Mrs.

Swain took us two little children to a small Presbyterian church in town they, themselves, gradually became more and more active in that very same church through the years until the two of them finally matured into very prominent leaders in that congregation. I sincerely feel that I eventually chose the Christian ministry as my primary vocational profession because of Martha Swain's concern for my spiritual development early in my life. That ministerial path I eventually chose is one I have lovingly followed for the past 66 years. Martha's revelation to Virginia and me gives special meaning to the beautiful passage in the Bible which says: "A child shall lead them." In my case my little sister and I were leading the Swains in their own spiritual development without any personal knowledge on our part that we were doing so. My religious path started with my saintly grandmother Anderson and continues to this day through Virginia and me, our five children, our 14 grandchildren, and our six great-grandchildren.

5

Leaving my borrowed home and re-entering my real one.

My sister Judy and I spent three years living with the Swain family. While there were melancholy moments for me on their 40-acre farm, there were also happy, sometimes scary, and certainly challenging moments for me as well. I will never forget the howling coyote sounds late at night when I had to make the scary trip to the out-house in back of the big house to go to the bathroom. I had a large Folger coffee can under my bed in case I had to 'make water' at night but sometimes the coffee can simply would not do the job for me. I knew I sometimes had to face the long path to the outhouse . . . and those howling coyotes. There were several times I wondered to myself whether it would be much safer for me to just sit there in the out-house after I had 'finished my business' until the sun came up in the morning rather than to try to make my way back to the house in the darkness with those howling coyotes nipping at my heels. The simple truth was that I did not have any pockets in my pajamas with rocks stuffed in them to scare those coyotes away. Each time I opened the out-house door and decided to run for it, I covered those 50 yards between the out-house and the big house in record time. I would breathlessly open the screen door to the back porch and slam it shut behind me. Herb Swain would always call out: "Is that you, Larry?" And, I would always answer: "Yes sir. It is." It truly felt as if I was still breathing heavily at the breakfast table the following morning.

More than being mostly bothered in those three years on the farm by fear I was more bothered by a profound sense of melancholy and sadness. The Swains were good people and their older sons who would never play with me or allow me to use any of their toys were not bad people. They were just older and, more than anything else, they just simply tolerated my presence. The sense of just being tolerated is a pretty heavy weight for a little boy to carry around within himself for three years. I was just lonely and melancholy for three years because I simply wanted to go home. I knew I would be greatly loved in my old home, not just tolerated. I remember that several times in a week I would go outside after the stars came out in the sky and I would look up into the heavens and repeat that same poem I had heard and memorized from some source I can no longer remember. Those words almost always expressed how much I missed home and how I wished my parents would come and get me and take me home to my real home. For three years they did not come but I continued praying and reciting those sad words to the stars above me.

Before I left the farm I was finally able to learn how to pull milk from the cows' teats. I remember the shiny silver bucket we collected the white milk in when I finally mastered the art of milking those wonderful animals. I remember the sound of the milk hitting the bottom of that silver metal bucket and me saying: "I did it! I finally did it!" There was no one in the barn with that cow and me except Mr. Swain. I had a big smile on my face and I looked over at Mr. Swain. His smile was even bigger than mine!

I was told shortly after that milking success that this was going to be a very big day for me. This was the day my mother and father were coming to get me and Judy and take us back to our original home. "I guess I milked that cow just in time, " I thought to myself. I went to the front porch of the house to look down the long gravel road for any sign of their arrival. This was the same mile-long road I walked home on each school-day from my one-room schoolhouse. I hoped there were no coyotes to greet them as they often did me when I walked down that road from school each day. I was sure my mother and father did not have any rocks in their pockets to chase the coyotes away as I had in mine when I walked home on that road. Sure enough, far off in the distance I saw two people walking in our direction. When they were half way to our country house I could see that one of them was a man and the other was a woman. As they got closer I assumed they were my parents but soon they got close enough for me to see their faces and they looked very different from the way I remembered them appearing three years earlier. The man was almost completely bald. My dad's hair had once been dark black and very curly as I remembered him looking three years earlier. It had also been very thick and bushy on top. I later learned from him that he thought it was the stress of the war which took all his hair away. My mother looked so much older and more tired than I remembered her looking before. It was going to take some time, I thought, for us all to get reacquainted with one another again. However, I was really ready for that time to begin. All my clothes and accumulated toys were packed in a large duffel-bag. Judy had her bag packed as well. My parents climbed the stairs to the front porch where I was standing and each one, in turn, took me in their arms without saying a word and hugged me. The first thing they said to me was: "Larry, you have grown so tall!" I was trembling inside and my face was all wet from my tears. I didn't want to let go of them so I just hung on to them for the longest time. I was thinking to myself that I had finally gotten the wish I had prayed for under the stars each night. The Swains were ready to take us in their old Ford car to the Greyhound bus station where we would catch our ride to our new home. I didn't at all fully understand this exciting moment through the adult eyes that were present on that day. It was surely a time of wonderful recovery for my parents but it must have been a time of enormous loss for the Swains at the same time. For three years the lives of these two sets of parents were tossed upside down and re-arranged. Neither home would ever be quite the same again for either of them. How could this little eight-year old child think about or even begin to understand what these adult farming parents were thinking? I wouldn't understand for many many years what they must have been thinking and feeling on that porch so many long years ago. I am only beginning to understand those feelings by forcing myself to write these words down on paper today. Clarity and understanding often takes time. A lot of it!

I was instantly confronted and surprised with how different the new world was that I was re-entering when I compared it to the old world I was leaving. There was the most obvious physical differences, of course, between the very quiet, rural world of cows, horses, pigs and chickens and the bustling urban world of busses, honking automobiles, crowded housing projects and the varied images of mix-raced people that looked so different to me than what I experienced in those three earlier years on the farm. There were no coyotes I had to throw rocks at in my new home and there was no big red shed where I had the room and time to dream and fantasize about riding around in my speeding race car. In my country home there were three boys and one girl that made up the inner circle of children as my intimate family. In my city home there were three girls and one boy that completed that inner circle. I quickly realized how great the changes were that had taken place in my three sisters and myself in those three years we were separated from each other and how much we had to learn and unlearn about one another in the days ahead. I learned right away that I was to become the big brother in charge of the three girls again. It had been some time since that had been the case.

There was no real place on the farm for me as a big brother. Mr. and Mrs. Swain took care of that matter as far as little Judy was concerned. I wasn't really that good at being a big brother earlier in my life and it was clear to me that I had a lot to learn in becoming a big brother once again.

It was not just the difference between country and city life that made me so unsettled in my return to my new home with my parents. As I just said, I did not realize until I returned home just how much I had changed as a person in those three years and yet in some important ways how very much the same person I still was as well. I had always been shy and somewhat quiet as a child. These characteristics seemed to have been amplified in me in those three intervening years I was away on the farm. In my new home there were less spaces in which I could find the solitude I was able to find on the farm. Six people living in a very small apartment found us constantly bumping into one another, violating what each one of us thought was their own private space. I had not paid much attention to the fact that new habits of behavior had taken hold within me in those past few years away from my parents and my other two sisters. Many of these habits and social preferences I had learned on the farm were out of sync with those of my biological parents. My parents smoked cigarettes, the Swains did not. My parents smoked so many cigarettes each day that they were seldom without one smoldering in their mouth. All of this meant that our very little and crowded apartment was constantly filled with smoke. I never got used to it and I hated the smell of the offensive odor that permeated our clothes, our hair, our bedroom linens, and our lungs. Every opportunity I had to be outside our apartment, I took it. My parents also drank alcohol. The Swains did not drink alcohol. My parents drank a great deal of alcohol and smoking and drinking alcohol made up a large part of what they did when they invited people over to the house to visit them on the weekends. Sleeping in very late on Sunday mornings were my parents' habitual responses to the hangovers they experienced from drinking to excess the night before. My habitual response to all of this, however, was to quietly dress in my best clothes on Sunday morning and to walk, alone, to the nearest church I could find for Sunday School. This very independent exercise of will on my part provided me a link not only to the little Presbyterian church that gave me my earliest serious spiritual education but it also helped me to keep alive the memory of my foster parents who had the wisdom and concern for my spiritual well-being by taking me to that little church in the first place. My parents never objected to this decision of mine to launch out on my own on Sunday mornings to find a church at which to worship and it was an activity I looked forward to and continued all through my childhood. None of my sisters cared to join me in this endeavor until many years later they finally joined me in church when they were in high-school.

We moved a little later to an area in the city of Tacoma called 'the Projects.' The Projects was a very poor section of the city that was located at the edge of town. People of all races lived there. One of the very special features of living where we did was that all of the land outside of the Projects was undeveloped land. There was forest-land and meadow-land mingled together. There were ponds of water and small streams with fish in them. It was a great place for children to wander for hours throughout the forest and to climb majestic trees where tree-houses could quickly and crudely be constructed. We children entered into great wars with one another by using the giant ferns as weapons which grew under the forest trees. These ferns quickly became spears in the creative hands of the little boys who stripped the little branches off their stems so they could throw these spears at their imagined enemies in combat. This forest-land was a place where we could play for hours and hours chasing and slaying our friends using these giant spears in mock confrontations with one another. Great strategies of warfare were plotted and executed that could never have been taught to us in the curriculum offered at the elementary schools we all attended. Following these sweaty encounters we mighty warriors would go deeper into the forest where we knew a cool pond was located. Without any encouragement from anyone else, we boys would strip off our soiled clothing and jump into the pond, buck-naked. How sweet were the rewards of victory after our successful warfare with one another. The entire world seemed at peace to us once more. We had made it so through our mock warfare! A little bit of the peaceful and exciting spirit of discovery on the farm flooded over me once again. I remember with so much fondness the close friendships that were formed between some of those forest combatants and me. We found ourselves gravitating to doing many exploratory and some even slightly dangerous things that our parents would surely have said 'no' to had we asked them ahead of time for permission to do them.

One of those exploratory ventures involved a railroad track that was located within a couple hundred feet of our home in the Project. A few of my friends and I could not resist the allure of jumping on-board these slow-moving freight trains with their inviting flatbeds that lumbered by our home several times each day. We would do this with considerable regularity and we would ride the trains for miles and miles knowing that we could always jump off the train and then we could catch another train back home later on in the day. We would time our jumping from the train to a place where we knew an encampment for men was located nearby. These men in the encampment were also riding the rails as we had chosen to do but they were not doing it for fun as we were doing. They were riding the rails to make their way from one work opportunity in one city to another job in another city. We called these encampments 'Hobo camps' because we had heard our parents refer to the men who lived there as being: 'Hoboes.' We did not think of this as being a bad name for these men at all. To us, this was simply who they were. They were called 'Hoboes.' We didn't think of that name as being disrespectful as we discovered later in life that it actually was a very disrespectful name. We would jump off the train near the encampment and walk through the woods until we smelled the smoke made by the big fire the Hoboes sat around to keep warm. The fire was the place where they could also heat their cans of beans or other canned goods to eat and to talk to one another about where the best jobs could be found to make some money. We would quietly slip into the encampment and listen at the edge of the clearing for a few minutes to the adult conversation and then very slowly slip closer to the fire and then finally we would sit down and begin to talk with the

Hoboes. The men (there were never any women in the encampment) would always offer to share with us some of the food they were eating. There was never any feeling of alarm on our part while we were visiting with these traveling men. They were extremely friendly to us young sojourners and always reminded us to be very careful as we jumped on the train for our return home. After several trips to the Hobo encampment we would greet those men by their first names we remembered from our previous visits and they would call us by our correct first names as well. After several visits with them it began to feel as if some of these men were slowly becoming a part of our extended family and over time we actually felt closer to some of them than we did to many of our own uncles we seldom saw or talked to. These venturesome experiences I had with my young friends were some of the warmest and most-cherished experiences of my entire childhood. I never shared the stories of these train rides and our Hobo visitations with my parents until many years later because I knew my parents would have dis-allowed me to continue these so-called dangerous explorations any longer. I did not tell them because I did not want these moments with my Hobo friends to end. This was an end I knew would quickly come to me if I had talked to anyone but my forest friends about them. "That's what friends are for" I thought to myself. "Friends are people we can swim buck-naked with and even take dangerous journeys to visit and talk with so-called social outcasts" I mused to myself.

6

Difficult talks in my home about the Big War.

As I grew older I was naturally very curious about the war that had taken my father away from our family for more than three years. My parents referred to it as 'the Big War.' It was more formally referred to as World War II. I did not know, in those early years as a child, that there actually had been a World War I. What I was increasingly most concerned about was what had taken place in my father's personal life during those war years. For the longest time I was never able to extract too much information from my dad about those frightful years and what had transpired in his life during that three-year period of time. He simply did not want to talk much about it. I came to know later as a teenager that he was a part of the 36th Infantry Division in the Army. This division had fought through northern Africa and all of Italy, Belgium, France, and Germany. Dad was involved in the famous 'Battle of the Bulge' conflict in Belgium that took place from December of 1944 to January 1945. There were very few people in his particular fighting unit in the 36th Division that survived that terrible battle. He was one of those fortunate few! The destruction in human and emotional terms was horrific and dad simply did not want to talk much about that to anyone, even to me. As I stated earlier, he had gone to war three years earlier with long, thick, black, curly hair and had returned home almost completely bald and gray. For a few years after his return he would sometimes wake up at night screaming and crying and on one very scary occasion he even began choking my mother in the middle of his sleep. These were episodes brought on by the terror and fright of those years of terrible killing and fighting he was exposed to.

After a few years following the war he did come around to describing a few events that he was involved in during those war years. One event he shared with me centered on him saving the lives of several of his comrades who were trapped by the enemy in the middle of a small German town. His friends and comrades were pinned down by the Germans with no way for them to escape. My father described to me how, in the midst of this frightening struggle with the enemy, he found a big truck abandoned with the key still in the ignition and he drove it into the middle of the intense fighting with bullets flying toward him from the enemy soldiers, riddling the truck he was driving. At great personal peril to his own life he was able to rescue 15 American soldiers without a single soldier being killed or wounded. The odds against his success in accomplishing this feat were very great. His efforts were even more astonishing when it was later explained to me by my father that he did not even know how to drive a truck. He explained to me that he just turned the key on in the truck and put the gearshift into some gear until the truck started moving. God, and perhaps lady luck, took him the rest of the way. He was later told by his superior officer that he was submitting his name to receive the silver star for his valor. Unfortunately, this same officer who gave him this information was later killed in battle and thus no one survived this particular war effort to write the commendation for dad's silver star. Of course my dad was always a hero to me and certainly to those 15 soldiers, but for so many years I wished that he had received that silver medal so that everyone else would know what I already knew about my heroic dad.

On another occasion a young Second Lieutenant, who had just arrived from Officer Candidate School in the States, ordered my father (who was a sergeant at the time) in the midst of a terrible battle with the Germans to go to the top of a nearby hill where a single small tree was located. This superior officer wanted dad to spy out the enemy from behind that tree so they could know how best to attack them. Dad said that any other place than that solitary tree would be a far better observation point as the enemy would already have had that tree location carefully measured and calibrated for artillery fire should someone be so stupid as to stand behind that tree to observe things from that location. The young and inexperienced Lieutenant ordered him to go to the tree anyway and he said to my father that he would court-martial him if he did not obey his orders. Dad told him that he would then have to court-martial him because he was not going to go up the hill to that tree location. The Lieutenant then said to my father: "Okay then, I'll go." He hurried up to the tree at the top of the hill and took his position behind it. Immediately, the loud whine of an artillery shell flew over the American soldiers' heads below and collided with the tree, blowing up the tree and the young Lieutenant into a thousand small pieces. No one in dad's fighting unit felt very good about that on that day. The arrogance that sometimes accompanies ignorance can often lead to terrible consequences. It certainly did on that awful day.

A few weeks following that fateful terrible event, my father described to me one of his most sickening experiences of the entire war for him.

He was running across an open field with his men while being strafed by enemy gunfire. They were trying to hurry for some safe cover from all the flying bullets around them. He saw a big log a few yards ahead and dove for cover behind it. His rifle, with his bayonet fixed to the end of it, rammed itself into the log as he dove for safety. What my father found out in that awful moment was that this big log was not a big log at all. It turned out to be the swollen carcass of a dead cow. All of the penned up and stored gasses inside the cow's body spilled out all over my dad's body. The putrefied scene was more than dad's stomach could bear and he began to vomit uncontrollably. My father told me that he completely forgot the enemy in the midst of that scary and awful moment. The exact words dad said to me were: "Larry, I simply puked my guts out and I thought to myself: to hell with the bullets and to hell with the Germans. I needed to empty my stomach of all its contents right now, bullets or not." So, dad stood up and for several gut-wrenching moments he vomited out the full contents of his stomach on the ground. He confessed to me that it was the worst day of the entire war as far as he was concerned. That picture is still indelibly imprinted on my mind after all of these years. Someone once said: "War is hell!" Episodes like these in my dad's life helped me to more clearly understand the profound truth of that remark.

A final war experience that was shared with me by my father was far more warm and humane but one which started out with all the possibility of being very cruel and quite inhumane. My father was sent out by his superior officer with a small group of soldiers toward the end of the war in Germany to complete a very inhumane task.

They were ordered to round up any German soldiers that were wandering around in the woods separated from their own fighting troops. They were told to arrest them but to not bring them back to the army prison camp that was already too full of previously captured German soldiers. The order was implicitly clear: they were not to round them up but they were to kill them. In that way they didn't have to feed and clothe and care for more prisoners of war. That command was highly repugnant to my father. It wasn't long before dad crept up close behind a lone German soldier who was seated, leaning against a tree, cutting his toenails with his nail-clipper. In that same moment this young German fighter was looking at a small picture he had removed from his wallet. It was a picture of his wife and two small children whom, of course, he was missing greatly. Dad, in telling me this story, said he could not help but think of his own family and how much he was missing them as well. In no way did he think he could kill this young soldier. Dad interrupted the young soldier's reverie by shouting: "Achtung!" ("Attention!") in a loud and frightening voice. The German soldier jumped quickly to attention, fearing for his life. My dad ordered him, in German, to give him his toenail clippers and to pick up his shoes and leave his rifle on the ground. Immediately, he said to the German: "Mach raus, snell!" which means: "Get out of here, fast!" That barefoot, young German broke all speed records as he disappeared from that forest with his heart beating rapidly I am sure. It was clearly the most fortunate day in that young man's life. Thinking about my father's story, I can just imagine how this young German husband and father must have told and re-told this story to his loved ones who gathered around their family table in the years following the war. I am sure he must have explained how, for the insignificant price of a small pair of toenail clippers and an American soldier's compassion, his life was spared. I still have those toenail clippers today. They are in my dresser drawer next to my socks as a reminder of how fragile life can be and how these fragile lives can be sustained by a simple and loving gesture from a kind and compassionate person.

Many years later when I was in seminary as a young, 19-year old student, I visited my parents and sisters who were currently living in Germany as a part of dad's military service there in the Air Force. For an entire week we toured the area in Germany where he had fought for much of his time in The Great War. He took us to a little bridge in the countryside where he and several American soldiers had hunkered down underneath for a few hours to hide from the Germans who passed by overhead on that same little bridge just inches away from where they were all hiding. A short distance away from the bridge was an old broken-down barn. Dad said to me: "After the Germans left the bridge my friends and I were hiding under, we took refuge in what was left of that old nearby barn and we slept blissfully for the rest of the night. We were all dead tired. Forgive the pun." he said. "The snow was falling very hard in that area so we all cuddled real close to one another in the corner of the barn even though it did not have any roof left on the top of it anymore. It was the first sleep we had had in several days and we enjoyed every minute of it, even though we laughed at how we were cuddled as close to one another as young lovers."

We children quickly learned to not engage our father in conversations regarding matters of warfare because we sensed how much pain it caused him to talk openly about it. It still hurts me today to recall not just the painful tragedies of arm-to-arm combat that my father personally endured but just how much personal pain his wife and we four little children endured as well waiting for him to come home. Broken bones and broken hearts. Casualties of war. Hell, indeed, was exactly what war seemed to be to each one of us in our family regardless of what side of the Atlantic Ocean we spent the war years on!

7

Games and other rituals in my home.

The home that Virginia and my children experienced in their youth was very different from the one I experienced in one very important way. There are thousands of books in my home today on almost every subject one might imagine. There was only one book in my parents' home that I can remember. It was not the Holy Bible. It was the World Almanac. The World Almanac was the equivalent in the early 1940's of the use of Google computing today. Dad would buy a new copy of the Almanac every year and would discard the old copy when the new one was brought into our house. One of the ways we children discovered how we could happily interact with our father (apart from the war-time stories) was through various games we enjoyed playing with him in the evenings. After dinner we did not have various gaming devices that children enjoy today nor did we have television diversions as all children now have. While there were of course board games and puzzles we could enjoy playing with, what my sisters and I really enjoyed were the interactive games we could play with our parents. Mother was not usually very interested in such interactive games, however, dad was so it was with dad that we played these games. One of the two games we children liked the most to play was a game called: "Mother, may I?" Even though our father was directing the game he insisted on us calling the game: "Mother, may I?" not, "Father, may I?" The game started with a command, by father, to one of us children such as: "Mother says, stand on one foot." That would mean that that person would have to respond by standing on one foot, but first that person would have to ask father the question: "Mother, may I?" If that person stood on one foot without first asking father's permission, he or she would have to leave the game. So, we had to listen very carefully to the instructions dad gave us. He would gradually begin speaking his commands faster and faster and he would not always preface his command with the appropriate phrase: "Mother says, stand on one foot (or some other similar command)." So, if we stood on one foot when dad did not first tell us to do so by saying: "<u>Mother</u> says stand on one foot," we would also be out of the game. It is pretty easy to play this game successfully if the speaker issues commands very slowly but dad was focused on tricking everyone by speeding the tempo faster and faster as we played it. Of course, the younger children got mixed up pretty easily and were often easily tricked by dad. He was always happy to give them second or even third chances before they were finally removed from the game. It was always between Marlene, the oldest of the three girls, and me as to who would be left standing on our feet at the very end of the game. There was a lot of laughter and a lot of complaining by the little ones that dad was talking too fast. It was high sport for our father and we loved seeing him having so much fun playing those interactive games with us. We never ever saw him lose any hair while he was playing games with us as he certainly did during his fighting in the Second World War.

Dad loved learning (his I.Q. was 155 at that time) and he was intent in every way to see that we children loved learning so these interactive games were one of the main ways he pursued learning with us children. The second interaction game I loved dearly with Dad was when he would take out the World Almanac and quiz us on material he had exposed us to at an earlier time. He made a deal with us four children that we could stay up as late as we wanted to in the evening as long as we were able to successfully answer the questions he would ask from the big Almanac book. As I just said, these questions were drawn from the information he had taught us from the Almanac in the previous week. This learned information was the basis for the games we would play a week later. If we missed the answer to any question dad would ask us, we were given a second chance to get the question right. If we missed it for a second time then it would be off to bed for us. It was quite a challenge for us, especially for the younger ones. Dad, of course, gave the two younger children an extra chance each night because of their age. No special favors for us two older ones of course. It got so that most of the children could name every state in the United States in alphabetical order PLUS, we were able to recite all the capital cities in each of those 48 states as well. 48 states were the number of states we had in the United States at that particular time. Dad delighted in probing into areas of trivia from the World Almanac relating to such things as sporting events, famous buildings, state birds, state flowers and on and on. It is amazing how much of this information is still stored in my memory today from those evenings of learning with my sisters and father. I discovered how much fun learning could be when the teacher himself was filled with the kind of infectious enthusiasm for learning my father possessed. I truly believe that my love for teaching as a life-profession stemmed from these evenings of learning and fun that were disguised simply as an escape from having to go to bed at night for us children!

One of the family rituals that all of us engaged in together -- both parents and children -- occurred when we were not playing any games at all at night. Those were the nights when we all went to bed at the same time. Our family always went to bed early. Of course, as I just said, there were no television programs at that time to watch and the few radio programs like "Fibber McGee and Molly" and "Lum and Abner" were only a half hour long and were aired early in the evening. By 8:00 P.M., on most evenings, it was off to bed for all of us, both parents and children. As soon as we were snug in our beds, and our doors were left open so we could hear one another, mother would start singing one of the popular songs of the day. Mother had a beautiful voice and all of us loved hearing her sing. Dad?

Not so much. However, even though he could not carry a tune at all we teased him by telling him that he had great rhythm and could remember all of the words. That made us all laugh. Mother and dad knew all the words to all of the prevailing love songs of the day and it was not too long before we knew all of those words too. I still remember the words to those love songs of the 1930's and 1940's. Shortly after Virginia and I began dating many years later, Virginia one day said to me: "How do you know all of the words to those old love songs you are singing to me?" I explained to her the nightly ritual of all of us children joining our parents in singing those old love songs to each other while we were falling asleep. With mother singing beautifully in the background, one by one we four children would finally nod off to sleep leaving our parents singing those great old songs all by themselves. I had never heard of any other family sharing this kind of family ritual with one another until many years later I remembered hearing the Walton Family members on television speaking out loving words to one another as they themselves were going to bed at night. Some of these expressions of love were: "Goodnight, John-Boy." "Goodnight, Mary Ellen." "Goodnight, Grandpa." They would continue naming all of the family members' names until everyone on the list was acknowledged before they finally turned their bedroom lights off one by one and they all would all go to sleep for the night together. It seemed like such a loving and peaceful way for our family to end each day and of course it proved to be a great way for the Waltons' to end their television program each week as well. The Waltons said 'goodnight' with loving words. Our family did it with loving music!

8

The stern mother that lived with me in my home.

My sisters always felt that my mother loved me more than she loved them. They would often say to me that she punished them more than she punished me. My response to them was that they (my sisters) deserved the punishment more than I did, a comment my mother often made to them as well. I did not seem to have quite the rebellious streak my sisters had. I was more withdrawn and introspective and they were more fun-loving and daring in their play. They just seemed to run into many more obstacles with one another and with others for which they ended up being punished. My mother was a stern taskmaster around the house. However, she was just as stern with the outside world as well. When I told my mother one day that my school teacher pulled my hair in school that day, my mother said to me: "Come with me Larry. We're going to school and have a talk with your teacher!" I so wished I had not told her about the hair-pulling. I was so embarrassed with the anticipated no-holds-barred confrontation with my teacher that I knew we were about to have. My mother did not experience any such embarrassment I had with confrontations. We got to the classroom and fortunately all of the children had gone home. Only the teacher was in the room. There was no preamble to my mother's stern conversation with my teacher. She simply said to the teacher: "I do not ever want to hear of you putting your hand on my son again or you will have to deal with me personally." She pointed her finger at the teacher while she spoke, almost touching the tip of her nose as she did so. The teacher was speechless. "If you have anything corrective to say about my son, put it in writing and send it home with him to me. I'll do any punishing that is needed, not you." It was a moment of heavenly bliss for me following the dressing-down my mother gave Miss. Light that day. I was so glad mother was on my side on so many stressful public occasions I encountered. Miss. Light saw the light on that glorious day. That light never went out as long as Miss. Light was at the school.

And that period of time at our school for Miss. Light was not very long because early next year she was gone. The story which circulated around the school was that she had a drinking problem and that she was fired. Her replacement was a wonderful lady named Miss. Baker. She loved music and started a singing group for both boys and girls. She encouraged me to join the little choir she was forming and much to my surprise I found I loved it. I had a high soprano voice and it drew me closer to my mother who had a beautiful voice as well. Shortly after the little choir was formed, Miss. Baker notified all the singers that an all-city choir was being formed and that one child was going to be picked from each of the one hundred elementary schools in the city of Tacoma to be a part of a large, all-city choir. Several of the students in the choir auditioned for the privilege of representing our school in the all-city choir. I did not audition. I was far too shy to do such a thing as that. On the very day Miss. Baker was to turn in the name of our school's choir representative she pulled me aside and asked me why I had not talked to her about being selected for this honor. I told her I did not think I was good enough to be selected. "Nonsense!" she said to me. "I think you have a beautiful voice and I would like for you to be our school's representative." I could not believe my ears. I told my mother and she was thrilled. I told my mother that I would have to ride a bus one day a week across town for practice. I would have to do this for the next two months. Our family didn't have very much money in those days and I immediately thought the cost would mean that I would have to decline Miss. Baker's wonderful offer. "We'll figure a way to make it work." Mother immediately said to me: "We'll figure a way" she repeated again. For two months this nine-year old fifth grader rode all alone on the bus across the big city of Tacoma for choir practice. There were about 100 young singers in the choir. On the first day of practice the choirmaster notified the choir that within a couple of weeks he would be handing out short solo parts to be sung by three or four student singers. He also said there would be one long solo part to be sung by one of the choir members and his or her solo would be accompanied by the rest of the choir. The name of that grand solo piece was: "Lo, how a rose 'ere blooming." When the choir began practicing the song I immediately fell in love with it. I don't think I had ever heard any melody quite so beautiful in my whole life. During the practicing time the choirmaster walked among all the singers to hear how each singer was singing his or her part and how gifted each person was in singing this beautiful piece of music. Three weeks later, just before he dismissed us from practice, he made an announcement to the choir. He said: "I have made my choice for the soloist for our choral performance in a month. The person who will sing the solo part will be Larry Keene. I was totally dumbfounded! I did not know what to say.

Everyone in the choir applauded. I felt as if I was going to cry. I realized I had to continue showing the biggest smile I could ever make or I, indeed, would cry for sure. I smiled all the way home on the bus and up the street to our apartment and into the kitchen where my mother was standing... and I immediately burst forth in tears. I gripped my arms tightly around my mother's waist so I would not fall to the floor! "What's wrong, Larry?" she asked me and I told her and cried some more. It was one of the greatest moments in my young life at that time. There must have been at least 2000 people in the auditorium the night I sang about that wonderful rose. Both my mother and father found the change to ride the bus and were there to hear about that rose as well. I have heard that beautiful song sung hundreds of times since that moment in my youth but it has never sounded more beautiful to me than it did that night when it was sung by these young children. The soloist wasn't half bad either!

When I was about 12 years old I had saved up enough money from the newspaper route I had to buy a suit of clothes. I had never owned a man's suit before and I wanted to buy the suit without any help from either of my parents, so my mother gave me permission to go to the store and make this transaction, alone. When I arrived home from the store with my new suit in a large paper box my mother told me to put it on so she could see it. The suit looked wonderful from the front but what I could not see was the baggy backside my mother could clearly see. Apparently the salesman had pulled the baggy backside together with his hands making the suit look as if it fit perfectly on me from the front. "Come on, Larry, we're going back to the store to have a talk with the salesman." I thought to myself that this sounded so very much like the Miss. Light-experience a couple of years earlier and I did not want to have any part of it. I was <u>so</u> embarrassed once again! We arrived at the store and mother literally threw the paper box into the startled arms of the salesman. "Do you really call yourself a salesman?" my mother practically yelled at the man holding the box in his arms. "It is clear what you were trying to do to my son who had never ever bought a suit before in his life. You thought you could sell this suit without having to make any alterations at all and that would be the end of it. Well, I am telling you that you are not going to get away with it. You take my son back to the alteration room right now and make the necessary adjustments you need to make without any charges to him and I will be watching you while you are doing it." The three of us made our way back to the back of the store and the salesman nervously made the adjustments that needed to be made to the suit. I walked out of the store that day with a suit that fit like a glove and with the deep pride in a kind of mother I knew would protect us children come Hell or high water. My mother was fearless when it came to us children. I never felt that my mother's love for us children was ever very warm or sentimental but it was certainly completely reliable, durably strong, and always a little bit scary.

I hated the smell of cigarettes and the fact that my parents were so addicted to smoking. Mother often talked about what an expensive and filthy habit smoking was and that she did not want me or the girls to ever take up the awful smoking habit. I told her I never would. However, my mother never left things to chance when it was within her power to control the people around her to do what she thought was best for them. One day when I was about 14 years old she called me into our bathroom and told me she wanted me to smoke a cigarette she had prepared for me. She had put a dog hair and a piece of rubber band inside the prepared cigarette. I told her I hadn't been smoking secretly on the side even though all of my friends did smoke. I begged and begged her to not make me smoke that cigarette. She was relentless, however, because she did not want me to ever take up the habit of smoking that had so enslaved her since she was a very young girl. So, very reluctantly, I took a big puff on the cigarette to get the terrible ordeal over with. Immediately I began to vomit in the bathtub. My up-chucking took several minutes before it finally stopped. My mother's aversion-therapy session with me worked like a charm. That was the first puff from a cigarette I had ever taken in my life. I have not taken one since.

Miss. Light, the salesman at the men's clothing store, and I, all withered under the stern, over-the-top demands of my mother. My three sisters took up smoking when they left home a few years later (as an act of rebellion to 'finally get their way', I am sure). The three girls and both of my parents died much earlier than one would have expected they would have because of their terrible cigarette addiction. I have lived longer than any other Keene member in our entire extended family which includes all the family members born to the 12 siblings in my father's family and all the family members born to the 10 siblings in my mother's family. "Thank you, Mom, for that cigarette in the bathroom. It was one of the best gifts you could have ever given me . . . vomit and all!"

I inherited my tendencies for having migraine headaches from my mother. I have also passed on this terrible condition to my five children and to most of my 14 grandchildren as well. I remember my mother having to go into a darkened bedroom and to lie down with a cold, wet wash rag covering her eyes when she had her terrible migraine headaches. She stayed in that darkened room until the pain subsided. Sometimes it would take a couple of days for that to happen. I follow that same procedure myself today when those headaches come to me. My children and my grandchildren do the same thing as well. It is a condition that one has to pretty much take care of all by oneself. However, there was one terrible painful condition my mother suffered from which often needed my help to deal with. My mother had very bad circulation in her legs. She told me this condition was called 'Phlebitis.' It was a very painful condition resulting in poor blood flow to her legs and feet. Her feet and legs would sometimes swell to twice their normal size. I would sit at the end of the sofa on which she was resting and I would rub her legs for hours to increase her circulation and give her some welcomed relief. We never spoke many words during those times but it was a closeness we both came to cherish. I never saw my father rub her legs and the girls had neither the strength in their hands or the inclination to lend a helping hand. The task fell to me and it probably helped to soften my resentment for the aversion therapy she imposed on me in the bathroom. I also came to learn of the many physical maladies she suffered from since she was very young. In addition to her migraines and her phlebitis, she had an incurable kidney disease called 'Brite's disease'. Today it is referred to as 'Polycystic Kidney Disease.' It is a disease that is characterized by numerous cysts forming on the surface of her kidneys. When the cysts would burst inside her they would bleed causing excruciating pain in her abdomen. Between her regular migraine headaches, the constant phlebitis pain in her legs, and her unrelenting kidney attacks, my mother's life was one of continual suffering. Sitting on the sofa and rubbing her legs gave me the important time I needed to think about her physical condition and the very real possibility that her time with us children might not be as long as we would all like it to be. Those brooding thoughts by a very young teenager came to fulfillment just three short decades later. Mother died, far too soon, at

62 years of age. Finally out of pain but also finally gone from all of us . . . forever!

9

That special bond with my father in my home.

As grateful as I am for the protective care my mother gave me in those formative years of my life, there were probably more moments of tender closeness that I shared with my father. I remember one evening, late at night, my father came into my bedroom and sat down on the side of my bed and woke me up. "What's up, Dad?" I said to him, wiping my eyes awake. I noticed he had a big duffel-bag filled with clothes in his hand. I remembered that it was the same kind of duffel-bag he carried with him years before when he went away to war. "Where are you going, dad?" I said. "I have to go away for a while." he said. "Why?" I said. I remember recently hearing my parents quarreling loudly late at night after we children had gone to bed. There were angry arguments about how each of them had behaved during the war when they were separated from each other for three years. It was clearly an adult kind of talking and the best thing I could make myself do, since I couldn't make any sense of any of it, was to simply go to sleep when it started up each night. "Sometimes we just have to do things we don't want to do and this is just one of those things." Dad said to me. "I don't understand any of this." I said with tears streaming down my cheeks. "I don't understand much of it either, son. I hope I will be back soon." he said. "We will see." That was difficult information for me to swallow because I thought my Dad understood everything. How was he not able to explain to me what all of this meant? I could understand me not understanding things but I could not understand him not understanding things. He walked out of the room and I did not see him again for what seemed like ages. I think it was only weeks that he was gone but every day felt more painful to me than did the day before. And then, one day he walked in the door and he was home to stay. We never ever talked about it again! I never understood, in that moment, any more than I had understood before he left, but it was okay with me because Dad was home. The family was complete again and that was all that mattered.

As I got older, more and more experiences with my father took me outside and connected me to people and places that he must have somehow felt would influence my life in meaningful ways as an adult. Living in Washington State gave us the opportunity to live near and to associate intimately with many

Native Americans . . . indigenous people. My father was a man who was easy for people to love. He had a ready smile and he never looked down on certain kinds of people as some other people often did. He always treated every person he met with kindness and warmth. Not respecting other people whose background was different from his own was not something I ever saw my father do. A couple of his Native American friends asked him one day if he would like to join them in fishing for salmon in waters that were prohibited fishing for everyone except Native Americans. He told them he would be honored to watch them fish and asked them if he could bring his young son along to witness this awesome experience. He told them I was ten years old and would be respectful of the privilege they were offering us. "Yes, we would love for him to join us." they said to Dad. "We will pick you up at midnight tonight." his Native American friends told him. "Why so late to go fishing?" my father replied. "You will better understand when we are through fishing," his friends said. They picked us up at midnight and we drove to a marshland near a dam on the Columbia River. There were signs all over the fences surrounding the marshland with the words: "No Fishing Allowed." written on them. The men ignored the signs and we all climbed over the fence together. Finally, following the beam of light from the flashlights the three men carried, we reached a place where a small stream was located. I will never forget how clear the water was. The stream was about three feet wide and about two feet deep. My father noticed that the men had no fishing gear with them. No poles. No fishing line and hooks. No fishing bait. Nothing. "Where is all your fishing equipment you will need to catch the salmon?" Dad said. "Here is our equipment." his friend replied. He showed my father a three-foot long gaff-hook. It looked like a baseball bat with a big hook at the end of it. "Now watch how us Indians catch fish." the man said. They turned their flashlights on the little stream of water and what the light revealed to me that night completely stunned me. What I saw were dozens of large salmon treading water in the small stream. "They are sleeping." the Native-American man said. Each salmon must have been at least two and a half feet long. The girth of each salmon was five or six inches across the middle. What I remember from that night was that they were larger than any fish I had ever seen. The oldest of the three Native Americans said: "Watch how we carefully select the fish we want to remove from the stream. We do not want to take home any fish that has cuts or bruises on them. That is why we have this gaff-hook with us. We will slide the hook gently into the gills of the sleeping fish and we will slowly turn the fish over in the water so we can see all sides of the fish. If we do it correctly we will not awaken the fish while it is sleeping." After rolling several salmon over and over in the stream they picked out the three salmon they wanted to take home with them. When they had made their selection the next step in their fishing process was the most dramatic part of all. They gently inserted the gaff-hook into the selected fish's gills and gently pulled it out of the water and laid it, flopping, on the bank of the stream. Quickly, the other two men hit the fish on its head with the wooden part of the gaff-hook so it would not suffer from being out of the water. They put the dead salmon into a wet gunny sack for its ride home. This process was repeated two more times and we quietly made our way back home with the three large fish. No one spoke a single word all the way. It felt like a most serious and sacred moment to me. It must have felt like that to the others as well. When we got home I watched them gut the fish and then remove all the scales from these three beautiful salmon. Once again, all their work took place in total silence as they completed what seemed like to me a fitting end to the entire evening's sacred ritual of fishing. When their work was finished they finally spoke. They said to my father: "Roy, we are going to slice one-inch steaks for you to put in your freezer. These steaks should last you at least a couple of months. Your family will have the kind of food that only the richest of people can afford. We give you this salmon because you have treated us as if we were brothers. Real brothers take care of one other. That is why we are giving you the gift of this salmon." What a display of brotherly love that moment was to me. When I reflect on that special event in my childhood, I wish the whole world had seen and witnessed that sacred moment I enjoyed that night with my new Native American friends!

The Columbia River is one of the largest rivers in North America. It is 1243 miles long. It spans six miles across at the mouth of the river where it empties into the mighty Pacific Ocean. Shortly after our fishing trip with the Native American friends of my father, dad said to me: "Would you like to see where this mighty river begins?" "Wow!" I said to him. "I sure would." So, once again we jumped into our old Studebaker and headed east out of Washington State and into Canada to find where the great river began its journey to the ocean. After several days of travel we got as close to the river's beginning point as dad thought we could drive in the old Studebaker and he finally said to me: "We have to hike from here, Larry." I can no longer remember all of the details of that hike but I can remember that after much walking through beautiful wooded areas, Dad said to me in a hushed voice as if we were standing on holy ground once again: "We are very close now." We had been following a stream of water that was getting smaller and smaller as we walked. "I think we have gone far enough." my father said. "Do you think you can step across this little stream?" he said. "It is only about three-feet wide," I remarked. I took a couple of steps backward and ran as fast as I could toward the little stream and jumped as hard as I could jump for the other side. I rolled over and over on the bank as I landed on the other side. "You have just jumped across the Columbia River." Dad said.

"Do not forget this moment." he went on to say. "Other people may not believe it when you tell them about it some day. What you did here today you may even come to doubt yourself, as well, but I am here to tell you, Larry Keene, that you jumped over the Columbia River when you were ten years old." What a wonderful gift my father gave me on that 1500-mile trip to the starting place of the mighty Columbia River. I think I may be the only ten-year old person on earth that can make the marvelous claim my father was talking about that day. Thank you, dad for sharing that thrilling moment with me and through me with all my children, grandchildren, and great-grandchildren as well.

Dad, who left home a few weeks earlier, came home to me and the family with his duffle-bag just when I needed him the most. My little red 'ugly-duckling' tricycle I had in Seattle when

I was a little boy had finally been replaced by a thin-tired racing bike with three shifting gears for climbing and racing along all kinds of terrain. I would ride for twenty or thirty miles at a stretch on my wonderful three-speed bike. Shortly after dad came home I took the longest bike ride of my life. I needed time alone to think about dad and mother and their lives together. Things were not at all settled in my mind about the two of them. I rode twenty-five miles away from home in one day never giving any thought to the fact that if I rode twenty-five miles away from home that I would also have to ride twenty-five miles back home to where I started. It might have been okay for me if it hadn't rained, but it did rain. And, it was not just any gentle, sissy kind of rain either. It was a full-throated Washington-State kind of rain! Needless to say I was soaked to the skin and cold and miserable by the time I finally reached home. Dad dried me off and put me into bed. A couple of hours later a terrible pain in my side awakened me in the night. Dad told me with considerable authority in his voice that it was clearly time to go to the hospital to be checked out by a doctor. So, into the old Studebaker car mom, dad, and I went in the pouring rain. "Larry has a badly inflamed appendix." the doctor said to my parents. "He will need to have it removed tonight. It is about to burst." That seemed serious to me. "Couldn't they just give me some medicine?" I said to my parents. Dad took me in his arms and held me and said: "We have to do what the doctor is telling us to do. Mother and I will be standing right by your bed waiting for you when you wake up and I will not be leaving your side." The three of us cried and I felt better. I remember seeing dad there at the bedside just as he said he would be when they wheeled me back into my hospital room. I was so glad that he had returned home just in time, duffel-bag and all, for my big hospital performance. I could not imagine how I would have made it through the surgery if he had not been there. I knew my mother loved me but the bond between my father and me was very special and that night that closeness truly paid off for me. Fishing for salmon together, jumping the Columbia River together, and finally crying together in my moment of great fear and dread created a bond between the two of us that lasted until he silently slipped away from us, forever, many years later.

After the war years my father worked for about three years in a paper- recycling plant in Tacoma. It was a dead-end kind of job that did not have much of a future to it but it was work and people took any kind of work they could find in those post-war days. Both of my parents came from homes that were much larger than our small family of six people. However, a family of six was large enough that the money dad earned each month was never quite enough 'to make ends meet' as our mother used to quickly remind us when we did not eat all of the food that was on our plates. "Your father has to work very hard for us to be able to buy that food you are not willing to eat. Don't you know how hard it is to make ends meet?" she would so often say to us children. I never quite knew what 'ends' she was trying to meet and she never volunteered an explanation to me. Perhaps it had something to do with the 'starving children in China' she also made reference to when we wouldn't eat all of the food on our plates. I could never figure out what these starving children in China had to do with our making ends meet but I am sure they had some important connection in my mother's mind.

We could always tell when we were coming close to the end of the month. The end of the month was the time when our father would receive his paycheck. For that last week, before paycheck time, we would eat a porridge made up of white rice and raisins each night for dinner. Mother would put a little cinnamon, sugar, and milk on it and it was wonderfully delicious! We thought we must have been really well off to be able to have such wonderfully tasty food to eat at the end of each month. We discovered that none of our friends were so fortunately treated as we were. I didn't know for many years that this was the way my mother stretched our food budget to feed us all until we reached the end of the month. Rice and powdered milk were pretty cheap in those days and a bag of raisins would last us for many months. In those final days of each month we children would also join mother and father in scouring all of the pillows in the davenport and soft chairs in the living room for loose change that might have accidentally fallen out of our pockets into the spaces behind and underneath those pillows. That was when all of us children learned to pray for miracles. Every once in a while a stray quarter recovered beneath one of those pillows would lift all of our spirits very high and renew our appreciation for divine intervention.

Work wasn't providing dad any advancement opportunities and the salary was certainly inadequate for the expanding needs of his growing family. One day it occurred to him to pay a visit to the Army Air Force recruitment office in downtown Tacoma. His I.Q. score in his enlistment file records indicated that it was very

very high. The recruitment officer told my father that he was officer material and that the Air Force would be willing to send him to Officer Candidate School for training and that he would be granted a Second Lieutenant status shortly after completing this officer training. Without ever having achieved any higher education beyond that of high-school this seemed like the chance of a lifetime to Dad. He went home to talk the entire matter over with mother and her answer to him was quick, decisive, and to the point: "No way am I going to be the wife of an officer! No way am I going to suck up to those snobby bitches that are married to their snobby officer husbands." My mother left school in the eighth grade and immediately went to work. She had always felt inferior to people (especially other women) who had better educations than she had achieved. So, it was an open and shut case as far as Dad's future career as an Army Air Force officer was concerned. Mother was okay with his re-entering the military service as long as it was as an enlisted man and not as an officer. In this way she could surround herself with people whose background was more like her own. I have often wondered with his very high intelligence how he might have distinguished himself in the military service as an officer. As much as my parents quarreled with one another over certain matters, it was clear they loved each other and would do nothing to ever bring shame or embarrassment to the other if they could prevent it. My father's willingness to subordinate his own personal ambitions in favor of what he perceived to be my mother's deep and personal inadequacies was a great lesson in selfless living on his part. I have often wondered if I could have managed to have made the same decision being faced with a similar choice as his. I admit, I resented my mother for many years for being so selfish in prohibiting my father's career advancement in the military because of her own feeling of inadequacy. One of the great lessons I learned at that time came to me from an older man I came to know and respect. He said to me: "Larry, don't judge someone else's decisions until you have been fortunate enough to walk a mile in his or her shoes." I came to feel that that applied to my father's decision as well. My father's love and concern for my mother's feelings was far greater than his longing for an officer's position in the Army Air Force. Becoming a career person as an enlisted man in the armed service was going to be just fine for him. As far as he was concerned, that was going to be the perspective from which he was planning to move forward in both his marriage and in his career. It was also a pretty important gift to me as well as a good lesson to provide for us four children who were old enough to witness what was happening to their parents on this matter.

10

My search for home through secondary education

My public school experiences from junior high-school through high-school were especially troubling to me in one very important way. I never attended any public school for very long because my father's career in the Air Force caused him to be moved or transferred to new locations every year or so. This meant we were constantly moving from one residence to a new one every few months. It also meant the selling of all of our old, used furniture from our former residence and then having to purchase new, that is used, furniture for the house we would move into next. It also meant moving into a newly rented house or apartment again as well. It was always a rented dwelling. Never a home or house that we purchased or actually owned. It was always rented! And, of course, it meant the enrolling of all four of us children in new public schools in every new location. So, being Air Force 'brats' as we proudly referred to ourselves as being, created for us a constant stream of new places to live and to gather collections of new but always used furniture items to place in their temporary locations until they, once again, would be sold before we moved on to a new temporary home once more. And, in addition to all of this, we would be receiving a new set of short-term friends to get acquainted with all over again in this new location. But, before we received these new temporary friends we had to say 'goodbye' to all the old short-term friends we had to cast aside knowing that the same process would be repeated a few months later. As a result of our family's continual moving around the country I never had the luxury of forming long-lived friendships that lasted for any length of time. I remember once sharing this fact with my wife, Virginia, and she told me how she still has many friends she has enjoyed since kindergarten and the first grade. She went on to tell me that she had also lived in the very same house from her elementary school years well into her college years. And, additionally, she told me that her family never was forced to sell their old, treasured, furniture and then be forced to replace that treasured furniture with other old furniture a few months later. So, the houses we four Keene children lived in while we were growing up did not have long-time memories tucked away in their corners and in their special hiding places as most other children had. Neither did the furniture we placed in those corners and along the walls of our transient houses have worn places on them that took years to form and to give that used furniture a sense of our special Keene character to them. However, the saddest legacy all four of us children shared with one another was that none of us formed long-term friendships where individual names and personal stories would become hand-me-down-experiences that could have enriched and blessed us all throughout all our growing-up years. The short-term friends I possessed became like cut-flowers in a vase to me. Many of these friends were quite beautiful people but they were like cut-flower friends. They were like friends without any roots to them. They were like friends with whom I shared very little history. Our friendship had no roots, so to speak. They were present in my life for a few weeks or months and then they were gone. I would never see them or hear from them again. They were simply gone where transient memories quickly disappear. In a very short time new memories would be formed in our new neighborhood by the courtesy of the United States Air Force. We children never seriously questioned the rightness or wrongness of this fact for us. It was just the way things were. God bless America!

During my junior high-school days I lived in a low-class housing project in Long Beach, California. It was also my very first exposure to so many people from different racial backgrounds that outnumbered the white people like me and my family. I remember that most of my friends in those days were African-American or Hispanic young people. In fact, my first girlfriend was a girl named Maria Sanchez. We were walking home one day after school holding hands with each other when we encountered my mother, who was walking home from our neighborhood grocery store carrying a bag of groceries in her arms. My mother spotted us locked together hand in hand and making amorous conversation with one another. She was furious with the obvious affection we were showing each other. My mother was an extremely prejudiced person toward people from different racial backgrounds. "Larry Keene, what are you doing holding hands with that pepito?" she yelled at me. My mother did not know the Spanish language at all so she used the only Spanish word she could recall having heard before, so she used the word for 'little daddy' which seemed like such a strange word to speak to me in that embarrassing moment. I don't think I had ever seen my mother so angry before. Especially in public. I was more humiliated than

I had ever been before. To be shamed in front of my very first girlfriend by my very own mother was more than I thought I would ever have to endure from her. People walking along the sidewalk nearby stopped and looked and listened to the very uncomfortable spectacle unfolding in front of them. I wished I could just have vanished from sight but there was no way my mother would allow that to happen. She bore into me with a ferocity I had never witnessed from her before. "You get your butt home right now, Larry Keene, and I never ever want to see you with that girl again" my mother screamed at me. My crippled and broken spirit limped home and found refuge for the entire evening in my bedroom. My locked bedroom door did not even open to my mother's repeated entreaties for me to let her in. I ate no supper that night and slipped out of the house early in the morning without breakfast to find some temporary sanctuary at school. I never spoke to Maria again. Apparently her humiliation was as great as mine because she built a moat of protection around her so we would never ever have to talk to one another about that terrible sidewalk moment again. I do not remember any of my classmate's names during those two years I spent in junior high-school but I have never forgotten the name of Maria Sanchez and the fondness I felt toward her. Nor will I ever forget the unwanted shame and humiliation my mother showered on the two of us young lovers that day. She stripped us both of our dignity and self-worth as we stood with such happiness in the middle of our new lower-class, inter-racial, loving space in Long Beach, California.

We children finally received a welcome reprieve from our continuous moving trials when

I moved into high-school. In my freshman year while we were living in the multi-racial project in Long Beach, California, I began to attend the huge Polytechnic High-school in town. It had almost 3000 students who attended there. It was as multi-racial as was our own neighborhood project we lived in. Early in my first high-school year at Poly High my father was transferred by the Air Force to the state of Oregon to assume a brand new service assignment there. This was the first time in his entire career that he would not be stationed to serve on an Air Force base. He would now have a large office in downtown Medford, Oregon that was his work site. He was assigned to oversee the training of all the Air Force reserve personnel living in Southern, Oregon and Northern California. And, best of all, it would be a three-year assignment which would mean we would be able to keep living in our new (rented) house longer and to owning our new (but used) furniture longer and, most importantly, we would be able to keep our new friends a little longer as well. So, we moved north to Oregon State in a hurry and had to move temporarily just outside the town of Medford to another very small, but old, town called Jacksonville, Oregon. Jacksonville was one of the oldest towns in the entire state. We children were scheduled to enroll for a short time in their only school. It was a school of 123 students from Kindergarten through the 12th grade. I had never heard of such a school like that before. I had just moved from a high-school with almost 3000 students to a high-school where there were only about 40 students in it. Two of my classes had only two students in them. For me it was a culture-shock experience of major proportions. Dad informed us kids that this would only be a temporary schooling situation until the paper-work procedures could be processed by the Air Force to a new school for all of us just outside Medford. There was one feature, however, about our new little school that was very unique beyond the fact that it was just small. There were three floors in this square, brick building. The high-school was located on the top floor of this antiquated brick structure and the elementary and junior-high schools were located on the bottom two floors. Located on the top floor, as well, was their quite unusual fire escape. There was another fire escape just like it on the second floor as well. The fire escape was shaped in the form of a large metal tube that was about four feet in diameter and the tube spiraled in circles from a top-floor window to the ground below. The highlight of our week was when we were required to participate in a fire drill by jumping out of the fire-escape window on the top floor and throwing ourselves down the inside of the tube, sliding and screaming at the top of our voices as we slid down to the ground floor. It was just like going on one of the best rides at the circus as far as we students were concerned. The students on the second floor exited their floor in the same way and screamed all the way down to the ground just as the students above them had done. There were also secret moments during the week when some of us students would sneak into the tube unsupervised with a big piece of waxed paper tucked underneath our rear ends as we captured a free ride down the exciting fire-escape on our own. The wax paper was designed to make the fire-escape even more slippery so we could slide down even faster when we practiced again on the scheduled fire-drill day. After all, we thought to ourselves, we needed to get out of the fire very fast, didn't we? So, hence the wax paper and secret trips on our own were for the public good, we reasoned to ourselves. There were many things that this tiny little school did not have that the newer and larger schools in the state could brag about possessing but the one thing that our tiny little school did have that no other school in the entire state possessed was the most awesome fire-escape that any school kid could ever want or experience!

My experience at Poly High School in Long Beach, California was unique in several ways. First, it had 3000 students enrolled compared to the 40 high school students at the Jacksonville High-school where I was currently attending. Secondly, fully one-third of the student-body at Poly High came from either African-American or Hispanic homes. All the students in my new school were white children. Even though the Air-Force had been racially integrated for many years, my family had only white friends and harbored many prejudices toward minority people (actually, only my mother did). I remember being so surprised when I was around 10 years of age and had a group of about eight friends with whom I played every day. All of my friends were white kids except one. He was black. I remember one day when we boys went deep into the woods near our house to play, as we often did. We took off all of our clothes to skinny-dip in a small pool of water in the woods. My African-American friend named Bobby jumped into the pond completely naked like the rest of us did and what surprised me more than anything was that he was 'black all over his body.' I was so naive at that young age that I somehow just assumed that his face and hands would be the only part of him that would be black. I simply had no idea that he would be 'black all over!' Healthy racial awareness by our family was so poorly understood and practiced by my parents that terrible, ignorant, and degrading perceptions and statements were often part of the everyday conversations I heard from my mother and less often from my father. I remember how they casually referred to Brazil nuts as 'nigger-toes' because of their color and shape. We children also used that offensive language too without any thought or consideration that those words might be offensive or hurtful to someone. The hurtful treatment of African-Americans by white people came forcefully home to me when I was in high-school. The famous African-American Harlem Globetrotter basketball team came to our Southern Oregon town to play an exhibition basketball game with a group of professional basketball players recruited from within the southern part of the state. One team was to be made up of all black players and the other team was to be made up of all white players. All the people in the stands were white people. My immediate feeling when I walked into the building was that I was viewing a team from another country playing our hometown boys. When the game was over (which the white guys lost) the real drama of the night was just beginning to unfold. I discovered later that when the Globetrotter team tried to find lodging for the night for their team that they were turned away from every motel in our city and from every other motel in the dozen towns they approached in our entire county. They had to travel for many miles to another county before they finally found a motel that would give this black basketball team lodging for the night. It was the most powerful lesson on race relations I had learned to that point in my life. I later learned that at that time – the middle 1950's – black people and white people lived in two very different worlds in America and that we were not supposed to mix these two worlds together. And, furthermore, I also learned that the people who lived in the white world felt themselves to be definitely superior to those who lived in the other world. The thought of my experience in the orphanage came immediately to my mind. As much as I wanted to reach my sisters on the other side of the chain-linked fence I found that I could not break through to the other side. I could get close to my sisters and I could even touch them for a very few precious seconds, but I came to understand where my place was supposed to be and that it could not or would not ever be changed for me. I couldn't help but wonder if the black basketball players felt a lot like I once did on that day in the orphanage, locked in one world and isolated from the other one! Racial awareness was very different in Southern Oregon in 1954 than it was in Southern California in 1954.

The day soon came when our family moved from Jacksonville and our very awesome fire escape. Three miles outside the city of Medford was a little farming community called Central Point. A brand new high-school named Crater High School had just been built there. It was named after the marvelous volcanic lake located 50 miles away. Crater lake was 900 feet deep, the deepest lake in all the United States and one of the deepest lakes in the entire world. I was about to be enrolled in the new school's very first student body class. My head was in a bit of a blur. In the span of the last six brief weeks I had been enrolled in three different high schools. I couldn't help but wonder to myself if I would ever be able to make any sense out of geometry. I settled into my new school situation with great enthusiasm. All the paint smelled new, the grass was new, the teachers were of course all new, but most importantly all my student friends were new to me as well. It was a scary prospect having to make all my friendships in such a hurry but I was finally looking forward to doing more than just making new friends or polishing up the insides of an old, antiquated fire-escape!

One of the first friends I made in my new school was named Harry Mallon. Harry came from a very poor family like ours and because of his low status in the community and the fact that he had a pretty severe learning disability, Harry had trouble making friends or fitting in with the other students in our new school. I took him under my wing as a friend almost immediately upon checking in at Crater High. Harry was a good natured person even though things had to be explained several times to him before he finally understood what his course of action had to be in any given situation. He had only one parent and his mother seemed to be similarly afflicted as was Harry so I made a suggestion to my parents: "Can we allow Harry to move into our house for a few months to help him get adjusted to school and to life a little better? I don't have a brother and it would be good for me as well" I said to them. My parents replied: "We will check with Harry's mother and if it is alright with her it will be alright with us as well." It quickly became a done deal and there were smiles all around. Harry was much larger than I was so he protected me with his brawn and I protected him with my brains. It was a good deal for both of us. It was not always smooth sailing around our house, however, with Harry as our guest. This was especially true shortly after we had gone quail hunting together with our small shotguns we both owned. Harry was lucky enough to have killed a few quails but I had killed none. I told Harry he had to pluck and gut the birds so they could be eaten later on in the week and he said he would do that. I failed to repeat that admonition to him several times as I had learned to do with most other things I had urged him to do. I completely forgot about those quails until a terrible odor began to develop in our bedroom. "What is that terrible odor in our bedroom, Harry?" I asked him. "I don't know." he said to me. I began following my nose and my nose led me to our clothes closet and to the big Army jacket Harry owned. I looked inside the big pockets in the jacket and the pockets reeked with the terrible rotting odor of the quails Harry had killed several days earlier. The pockets were also filled with hundreds of maggots crawling all over the jacket. My parents were furious and ordered Harry to take the jacket outside and throw it in the garbage because it was beyond any possibility of being salvaged at this point. Both shotguns were confiscated from us and put into quarantine. Our hunting days were over for the time being.

Shortly after the quail incident the two of us thought that it would be fun to play hooky from school together for the day. Neither one of us had ever done that before and we thought it would be fun to find a place to go fishing and just chill out together for the day. We secretly packed a lunch and snuck off into the woods for a long hike to the place we knew where the fishing was great. However, what we thought was going to be fun turned out to not be so much fun at all. We began to remember stories we had heard about truant officers who roamed the woods and the countryside during the daytime for students who were skipping classes for the day. Those students who were arrested by those officers were brought to the school for punishment. For the life of me I don't know why these thoughts hadn't occurred to me sooner. So, we spent the entire day sneaking around the woods constantly looking over our shoulders for the truant officers that we expected were going to momentarily pounce on us and ruin our holiday. We were so worried and frightened we finally made our way home, glad to have not been discovered for our wayward actions. We had spent the entire day playing hide-and-go-seek with the school police, when we realized we hadn't eaten a single bite of the lunch we had prepared early in the morning. The next day we quickly became aware of the fact that we wouldn't be able to get back into our classes without a note from my father explaining our absences the day before from classes. I went to my father to confess our deviant act of the previous day and quickly realized that it might have been easier on us if we had just been caught by one of the truant officers the day before. The hurt and disappointment I saw in my father's eyes for what we had done was never to be forgotten. "If you had simply come to me and told me you would like to skip school for the day I would have probably said: 'Sure, go do it, but don't make a habit of it.' But, your sneaking around behind my back really disappoints me in you, Larry. Now I don't know if I can ever trust you anymore." I felt stabbed in the heart by his words. My father and I were very close and I, for the moment, had created a small space between us that wasn't there before. Could I ever reduce that space between us? I was too young to know the answer to that question for sure. I certainly hoped I could. I quickly realized I still had to ask him to write our two excuses for our re-admission to class. "Sure," dad said. "I will be happy to write your excuses." He got two separate pieces of paper, dated them, and began to write his excuse for me: "Please excuse Larry for he played hooky with Harry yesterday." He then took the other piece of paper and wrote: "Please excuse Harry for he played hooky with Larry yesterday." "Dad," I said to him, "You can't write that!" Dad said to me: "Do you want me to lie to the school official, Larry?" Of course I did not want him to do that but I felt mortified to have to face the school official in a few minutes with those words written by my father. The fact that I had to openly confess where Harry and I had spent the day before and to have my father help rub our noses into our foolish infraction was almost more than I could bear. The end to our wandering off the path of good behavior was not at all what I had expected it to be. When the school official opened both notes from my father and read what he had written about what Harry and I had done the day before, he broke out with the biggest laugh I had ever heard this quiet and reserved man ever make. He said: "In all my years at this school I have never read anything so refreshingly honest before." Looking at Harry and me trembling before him, he said: "It looks like you have suffered enough. You can go to class now."

Scholarship had always been my greatest interest and preoccupation in school. If anything had to do with reading or writing assignments I was more than up for it. I greatly enjoyed studying. It was like breathing for me. Good grades did not come easy for me. Good grades took a lot of work and perseverance on my part but I loved having to make the effort to earn those good grades. That enthusiastic response of mine to the challenge of learning started on the first day of my entering the first grade and did not end until my final day in graduate school many years later. So I began my first day at Crater High-school just the way I did every day at every other school I ever entered in my life: by hitting the books. I continued doing just that until our athletic coach, Mr. Schwartz, stopped me one day after gym class and said to me: "I have noticed how smoothly you run around the track during class. Have you ever thought about coming out for the school track team? I think you could become quite a fine runner, especially the running of the longer distances. I do think the mile event would be a great race for you!" I had always been a skinny kid and never thought there would be any place in sports for me. But, if Coach Schwartz thought that there was life in sports for skinny Larry Keene then I was going to give it a try. And, try I did. I competed for a spot as one of the milers on the team and I finally made the team. Being a very competitive person, I practiced and practiced until I became the best miler on the school's track team. Before I graduated from Crater High I set our school record for the mile event by running it in the time of four minutes and 50 seconds. Not too bad for a very skinny guy. I discovered that a person could not only open themselves to books and other academic pursuits when they entered the school environs but they could also open themselves up to many other exciting opportunities for themselves as well. I quickly discovered that a mile runner is not just a person going around in circles when they were running around the track at school. Sometimes they are actually going somewhere very important. I found out that in school one can hit the books and hit the track together at the same time and learn something important and life-enhancing from each of them. I also learned that one doesn't have to set a school record while enjoying all of these life-enhancing experiences. One can become quite successful in life by filling oneself with a sense of the joy that comes from doing something a person might not have ever thought they could do . . . until they actually tried to do it!

    I learned that great truth more fully in my second year at my new school. I was competing in the mile run in the big district track meet where I was favored to win that race. One lap around the four-lap race track I knew there was something terribly wrong inside me. Right near my appendix scar on my right side I felt an excruciating pain. I tried to push on through the pain but it was getting worse not better. I was too humiliated to pull out of the race seeing as I was the favored runner in the race. I finally realized that I could no longer take any more of that pain so I pulled off of the track onto the grassy field in the middle of the large oval track. A thousand fans were all witnesses to my public humiliation. I wished the ground would somehow just swallow me up and not leave any hint of my personal disgrace I felt within me. Such a merciful intervention by the Almighty would have been a wonderful gift in that moment but it looked as if the Good Lord wasn't going to make a divine visit to me on that day as I continued walking around in the middle of the field to diminish my pain as well as to hide some of my shame for having to give up my race in front so many people. I finally noticed my father, who had been sitting in the stands watching the race, slip out of his seat and begin to run toward me as fast as he could possibly run. In an instant his big strong hands wrapped themselves around me and pulled me close to his body while I sunk, dejected, into his arms in tears. "I'm sorry Dad, I didn't want to disappoint you" I said to him. "You have never ever been a disappointment to me Larry and you are not a disappointment to me now." he said. "This is not your fault. It could have happened to anyone and I am so proud of how you were able to keep on going even though you were in such great pain. You will live again to race once more and I will be right there on that day to watch you do it." I had the greatest dad in the whole world and on that day and in that moment I knew the truth of that wonderful fact.

There was not a shadow of a doubt in my mind about that truth. I came to understand in that moment that some lessons in life are learned not by succeeding but by failing. Sometimes our failures help us see some things more clearly than do the successes we experience in life. Like, for instance, having a father that will willingly stand next to you in your moment of abject humiliation and shame. Those hundreds of spectators in the stands finally went to their homes that day and I was never to see or feel their presence again but dad stayed there with me that afternoon until I was ready to leave with my lingering pain. At first I was greatly disappointed that I was not bringing my coveted and longed-for trophy home with me. That is, I was disappointed until I realized that I was actually bringing something home with me that I prized even more highly than that bronze trophy prize for winning that race. I was bringing my loving and supportive father home with me. He also helped me to bring home my dignity as well. My dad and my dignity. No better trophies in life than that!

Earning athletic letters for participating on both the track and basketball teams for three years at Crater High were enormously exciting accomplishments for me in high-school. However, it was my academic pursuits in school that brought me my greatest joy while I was there. I was fortunate to have graduated near the very top of my class and was privileged to have been selected by the school to deliver the Valedictory address the night of my graduation. I remember titling my speech: "Fides in nostro futuro." The Latin translation for my speech was: "Faith in our future." From starting out his life as a young child in a very poor family and then being sent to an orphanage and to a foster home for three years, one can guess just how much I depended on faith to propel me into my future. So, I wanted to share some of that faith perspective with my classmates and guests that night. I had previously told my classmates that I had decided to enter the Christian ministry as my chosen profession in life. Several months later, after I had entered college for my pre-ministerial training, I received a wonderful letter from my high school inviting me to return to the high school at my leisure to address a public assembly of the entire student-body to explain to them just why I had made my choice to enter the Christian ministry. Apparently no other student who had ever attended Crater High School had ever made a similar choice and the school officials wanted me to return and share with my classmates my thoughts on having made that decision for my life's vocation. Weeks later when I entered the large high-school auditorium to speak to them, the entire student body enthusiastically stood up and applauded my arrival when I entered the large auditorium. Deep inside me I felt so emotional because I was so happy with the reception they gave me. I refrained from crying (which I wanted to do) because at the time I thought that it wouldn't have looked very ministerial of me to have done so. If I had it to do all over again today I think I would have let the tears flow freely down my face in that moment because I now think that it would have looked more human of me to have been more open with my feelings. But, of course, what does a 17-year old young person know about these sorts of things?

11

College life, a new kind of home for me.

As I said previously, my mother had 9 siblings in her family and my father had 11 siblings in his. None of those 22 children ever attended college in their lifetimes. Nor had any of their many children ever attended college either. I was the first person from our entire extended family tree to have had the privilege of enrolling in college. As I look back on my life, pursuing my educational objectives was my primary motivational interest all along the way as I matured in Washington State, Southern California, and finally in Southern Oregon. In school, the excitement of learning and my competitive drive to always be at the academic top of my school class, challenged me from my very beginning in that little one-room schoolhouse to the end of my formal education in graduate school. I think one of my principle motivations behind becoming a university professor was my unwillingness to move away from the thrilling and satisfying learning environment that the university world of teaching and learning continued to provide me. I don't think I ever enrolled in a single college class of mine that I did not enjoy or profit from in some meaningful way. I can honestly say that even those courses that were taught by poor instructors were experienced by me as positive experiences. It had been my conviction throughout my educational journey that the responsibility for learning lies more with the student than with the teacher himself or herself. It has been my feeling that even a poor teacher can teach a truly motivated student something important or valuable. However, it is also true that if a student is not motivated to be an eager learner even the very best teacher in the world will not be able to teach that student very much.

When I was 16 years old and about to graduate from high-school, I announced to my parents that I had made my decision to enter the Christian ministry. I informed them that in the fall of that year I was going to enter a small Bible college in northern California to become a minister in training. My parents were not surprised since I was very active in the small church I was currently attending and knew that several of my friends in my church had previously gone to that ministerial school as well. They were both thrilled with my decision and they encouraged me to pursue my dreams there if I wished to. Following that announcement to them I received a letter from Stanford University where I had also applied for inclusion in the Fall semester to enter a pre-law program of education. I had not told my parents that I had also submitted an application to Stanford, a school with a world-wide reputation of considerable renown. Now I had to inform them that I had received from Stanford a full four-year paid scholarship to one of the most prestigious universities in the entire United States and that it was a high honor for me to have received a scholarship of any kind let alone a four-year, all-tuition-paid one. I told them I was seriously considering accepting their offer. My father said nothing to me regarding what he thought about this action of mine but just quietly left the room we were sitting in. Later on in the day my mother explained to me that he was greatly hurt when he heard the announcement of my new intentions to possibly become a lawyer. He told my mother that he was so proud of the fact that I was giving my life to a life of spiritual service in the ministry and that no one in his entire family had ever chosen such a noble path to follow in life. He told her that he would never try to talk me out of becoming a lawyer but he revealed to her that he had been counting on me to follow through on my original dream for a life of spiritual service. I never understood how deeply my father had felt about the choice I had made for my life of spiritual work, especially since he had never shown any interest at all in attending church or to engage in any other spiritual pursuits. We had often talked with one another about my becoming a chaplain in the Air Force but I told him I did not want to be limited by serving within the boundaries of military life alone. Dad also knew of my pacifist leanings and how life in the military would make it more difficult to stay true to my commitment to save lives instead of taking them away. He understood that and encouraged me to be true to myself. How my father and mother felt about my life's vocational choice were very important to me. I knew I had to do some serious thinking about my Stanford scholarship and my little Bible college in northern California. After several days of prayerful deliberation I decided to give up the Stanford scholarship and enroll in San Jose Bible College, a small, unheralded school of only 150 students. I have never been sorry I made that choice. Neither were my parents.

Before I left for college my parents gave me a birthday party for my 17th birthday. It was my very first birthday party in my entire life. All my friends were there. Mother baked a delicious chocolate cake, my favorite kind. This was a very special moment for the entire family because within a few weeks I would be moving to California for college and mother and dad and the girls would be moving several thousand miles away to Bitburg, Germany. Dad was being stationed there for three years by the Air Force at a very large Air Force base where hundreds of fighter jets were located. This was to be a time of separation from one another once again. Separation from people I loved was to become a repetitive kind of experience in my life that would continue to define for me the kind of life I would so often have to face. Much of the time I had to face these separations alone. Even though I was much older now than I was when this separation time occurred to me for the very first time on the farm, I found that those old feelings of abandonment I felt when I was a young child were much closer to the surface of my heart than

I thought they would be. During the holiday vacation times in school like Thanksgiving, Christmas, and Spring Break when all the students at school went home to their families to visit, I remained behind at school in my room . . . alone. All the other students were gone. Even the cafeteria was closed and all their workers were gone as well. The janitors were gone too. It was just me locked down with my thoughts . . . very lonely ones. The feeling of being alone during those festive holiday moments, far from family, is difficult even yet to quite put into words. I felt I was too old to cry about it but I also felt I was just young enough to want to. Bottling my feelings up deep inside me became the way I chose to deal with those kinds of painful, lonely experiences in my life. I was always the person with the big winsome smile on his face so no one ever suspected that the 'outside Larry' was any different from the 'inside Larry.' But it was very much different on the inside and I knew it and I felt it. No one ever chose to ask me whether there was any difference between these two Larry's so I never volunteered any further information to them. That practice sometimes continues for me even to this present moment. I have found that it is simply easier for me sometimes to just make accommodations to life's painful circumstances by simply smiling at the world around me and moving on through those lonely and sometimes painful moments.

A very big part of my college experience was music. Since my very early experience in the all-city chorus in the fifth grade I have loved to sing. I joined every singing group I could find in each school I ever attended. When I enrolled in college my singing interests and talents enabled me to be selected to be a member of the esteemed college quartet at our school. Our quartet, the <u>Loyal Lordsmen,</u> sang at various churches around the state each weekend and at other public gatherings as well. We traveled all over the United States in the two years I sang in the school quartet and even recorded a long-playing record of sacred music while we were together. One of the side benefits of quartet participation on my part was that all my dress-up clothing for the quartet was purchased by the college and my school tuition was also paid for me by the school as well. That was particularly beneficial for me because my parents did not have any extra money to help me pay for my school tuition and rent. I worked part-time while I was in school and would even send several dollars of my own money home each month to help my parents meet their expanding financial needs at home. So, being able to sing on pitch with three other guys turned out to be a huge spiritual and financial blessing to me. We traveled each weekend with the college president to a different church location and we supplied the music and sermon for the morning and evening church services at the church on Sunday. The presence of four handsome(?) college students served as a powerful recruitment device to attract many students to enroll at our small Bible college. The other three members of the quartet did not particularly like the public-speaking part of the quartet responsibilities for the weekend so, even though I was the youngest member of the quartet, I was selected to be the spokesman for the group each week. By the time I finished my time with the quartet two years later I had written and delivered a couple hundred sermons to those churches we visited on the weekends. The numerous speaking opportunities gave me invaluable experience in developing the preaching skills every minister in training must possess before he or she would ever be hired by a church in an official capacity. That ability to feel comfortable standing in front of an audience and delivering an address before crowds of all sizes was, of course, one of the great benefits of my college education with the quartet. Whoever said: "Practice makes perfect" certainly described my situation perfectly. I would never say I was perfect in my preaching but I was certainly better than I would have been had I not had that tremendous experience singing and speaking on behalf of the college quartet.   Following my two years studying at the San Jose Bible College and singing with their college quartet, I transferred to the Cincinnati Bible Seminary in Ohio. It was a larger and academically demanding school. It was what I was needing at this stage in my life. I lost contact with my California quartet for a couple of years until we re-united for my wedding in 1957. The three quartet members served as my wedding attendants at my wedding. In fact, of the 1000 people who attended our wedding, only these three people and John Heberling, my best man, were <u>my</u> guests that evening. All the rest of our guests were Virginia's friends.. My mother was seriously ill at the time of our wedding and my sisters were living with my parents in Massachusetts, which was a long way away from Long Beach, California where the wedding was going to take place. Our wedding was to be held in the very large church building where Virginia's father was the minister. It was very sad not having anyone from my family at my wedding. My quartet friends: Richard, George and Dick, stood up for me on my wedding day

66 years ago. Our high tenor, George Caldwell died several years ago from pneumonia but Richard Palmer who is a retired high-school teacher and Dick Moore who is a retired pilot for Northwest Airlines, still are alive and happily married today. John Heberling, my best man in my wedding, just passed away a few weeks ago. He was 90 years old. My Virginia was the daughter of Reuben L. Anderson, the minister of the First Christian Church in Long Beach, California. His church was a very famous and historical church among the Christian Churches of America. It had a membership of approximately 3000 members. I never realized that the brown-eyed beauty I fell in love with at summer camp in 1955 was related to such a famous father. So, since Virginia was the first of the Anderson's six children to have gotten married, one would expect that the church would

be filled to the rafters for our wedding. And filled it certainly was. And four of those 1000 guests on that evening were my special friends as well

College life in the 1950's was a profoundly revolutionary and life-changing experience for me. Until those college moments in my life, my religious quest in life was mostly a very private one for me. While I attended and enjoyed my connection with my little church in Southern Oregon my family and relatives did not, for the most part, share in my religious culture and values at the time. My life experience as a young man was one in which my religious experience was wrapped up within a very secular culture as it is with most people. In the college period of my life, however, it was quite the opposite. Most of what I did every day took place within the religious context of the Bible college itself and the growing extended family of religious students, teachers, and religious friends. That was so opposite of the seventeen years I had experienced previously in my life. I was provided, in Bible college, a wonderful opportunity to redefine myself in a brand-new way. I saw myself as a budding religious scholar. In the first two years of my schooling I received all A's in all of my classes. I cannot deny that I loved it when I overheard students whisper among themselves: "Let's ask Larry. He'll know the right answers." I loved traveling with my three friends: George, Richard, and Dick in our college quartet. Traveling throughout the United States and becoming well known in most of the cities and towns of California as a singer and speaker helped to add a new definition of who I felt myself to be. In this earliest period of my adult life I adjusted to living a life of relative religious isolation. I was separated from my family and as a result of that I expanded for myself the world of my shyness where I felt the most comfortable when I was either alone or with a very small circle of close religious friends. But in the religious college I selected I found myself moving from a setting of isolation to one of insulation. In Bible college I was insulated in a world where everyone was just like every other person in that small religious world of mine. They dressed alike. They believed and thought alike. They ate and drank the same food and they did all of these things in the very same small-school setting. We all quickly developed the same language and vocabulary when we spoke to one another. What isolation and insulation have in common is that both are divorced from the wider world around them. They both develop a kind of blindness to the 'others' in the outside world from whom they have been distinguished and separated. These two social conditions which defined my earlier experiences in life were now about to be challenged by my new venture into my life's vocational choice - - the ministry.

12

Finding my home in the ministry.

I was selected at the end of my first year in Bible college to be the youth director at the First Church of Christ in San Fernando, California. This position was to last for the three summer months of 1955. "How good is this?" I thought to myself. "Be careful!" I heard myself saying to my inner self. Remember it says in the Bible: "Pride goeth before a fall." I knew that working with this youth group during the summer months had the potential to be the most stimulating learning experience of my life. The senior minister of the host church at that time had the reputation of being a very stern taskmaster. He was a carefully disciplined scholar with a no-

nonsense attitude toward what a young youth minister should be like. He abhorred the shallowness of poor preparation by youth leaders and strongly disapproved of those who relied more on style than substance in their efforts at youth leadership. After three months of what I thought was a fruitful period of growth for our youth program (we had grown from five young people in attendance to over fifty youth in attendance), I sat down in Rev. Applebury's office for a final review and evaluation of my summer's performance at the church. I was terrified to be sitting in front of a man who was so highly respected in the country both as an ordained minister and as a distinguished professor of Greek language and biblical studies at our local Bible college. The meeting was very short. His only comments were as follows: "While I have noticed much growth in the size of our youth program during the summer I am afraid you have relied more on your personality, Larry, to achieve this growth than upon other more sound principles that would have guaranteed that this growth would be sustained long after you have left to go back to school in a couple of weeks." I looked around his office for a hole I could crawl into but found that no such place existed in his office for me. I felt stung by what he said to me and was hurt more than I could ever put into words. I had expected one thing from my mentor and received something quite different from the good Reverend. I thanked him for his words and for the opportunity to have worked with the youth during the summer. I slipped quietly away from his office on rubbery legs that I was not sure would successfully carry me to the place I was temporarily calling 'home' in a church member's residence nearby. I phrased and re-phrased Mr. Aplelbury's words in my mind over and over again. After the third or fourth iteration of his words, some of the awful sting to my ego finally began to disappear from the bruising words spoken by my summer's mentor and I began to hear those spoken words for what Pastor Appelbury actually intended for them to be understood by me. I began to see them as words of caution and warning. I think he was trying to say to me: "Be careful that you don't let your ego get in your way as you seek to be a leader of people for God's sake." As initially hurtful as these words were to me, upon further reflection those words spoken by this elderly and wizened minister were exactly what I needed to hear after my heady accomplishments of that summer. I have given much of that same speech to hundreds of youth ministers and associates I have shepherded and mentored during my long ministry. Those words were the most painful words I have ever received from another person in critiquing my ministry over the years, however, they were the most helpful ones for me to hear as well. God placed this stern taskmaster squarely on my path just when I needed him the most. And as I have just said, I have been in his same position so many other times when I have had to face other young ministers while giving them the best critique of their ministry I could give them. I have tried to raise with them the same concerns this very loving elderly minister raised with me. I have always tried to say to them something like: "Our greatest enemy in our ministry is never going to be someone else. Our biggest problem will always be our own ego, not someone else's. Our greatest downfall will always come from some flaw within oneself not from some challenge coming from some person or place outside one's own self." I have learned that the spirit of Rev. Applebury lives on within me. Thank God for that!

My greatest take-away gift at that time came from that summer while working with those young people. I took 20 of those young people from our church to summer church camp where we spent a week learning about God and how our faith should be expressed and lived out in the world we live in. While I was there with these youth as a camp counselor I was cautioned that I should not make any romantic overtures toward any of the female campers while I was there. I even signed a pledge to behave myself in this regard. Of course it was easy for me to sign that document of agreement because the last thing in my mind was to do any romancing in our Christian camp. That worked very well for me until I saw Virginia Anderson, one of the graduating senior campers in camp. "Ginny", as all the other campers referred to her, entered the nurse's cabin one afternoon with two of her high-school girlfriends. I was just about to leave the nurse's cabin, having taken another person there for some minor first-aid he needed. The three very attractive female campers (who were actually my same age) stopped me and asked me if the nurse, who wasn't there at the time, had anything for chapped lips. I remember, of course, signing the agreement to not engage in any romancing while serving at camp as a counselor so I decided to not put myself in the dangerous situation of checking their lips out too carefully or closely. I stepped back a few feet from them and pointed out the cabinet across the room where a jar of Vaseline jelly was located and told them to put some of the Vaseline on their lips and that should do the trick of healing and moistening their lips for them. Two of the young ladies took a little of the jelly and spread it quite thinly and carefully on their lips. Virginia ('Ginny'), however. took quite a big glob of Vaseline jelly and spread it luxuriously all over her lips for maximum effect. To be quite frank and clear, it looked a little messy to me. However, it certainly got my attention for sure. I noticed her beautiful, brown eyes and the long, shiny, brown, pony-tail hanging down behind her. Did I mention that her gorgeously beautiful face stood out to me as well? I couldn't help but wonder to myself whether she had put the Vaseline on her lips the way she did on purpose to get me to take a longer and more careful look at her. "Surely not," I thought to myself. But I did, indeed, give her a second look and a third one too. I couldn't help but think that she was not only beautiful but she was pretty smart as well. "I have always wanted beautiful and smart children" I couldn't help but think to myself. "Watch out, Larry," I thought to myself. "Remember that signed document!" One week later that signed agreement for non-romancing behavior by us camp counselors was no longer in force because camp was over and behind us. So, I made it a point to gather at a local roller-skating rink where I knew many of the summer campers would be in attendance for a youth roller-skating party. I rented my roller-skates and began skating circles around the room. In high-school I did a great deal of roller-skating and had learned to skate backwards and do a lot of pretty impressive tricks on skates. After taking a couple of leisurely turns around the roller-rink I spotted Ginny and one of her girlfriends skating cautiously and very slowly around the roller-rink. It was clear to me that brown-eyed Ginny was not too sure on her feet in those very slippery skates. Her girlfriend, Nancy Angle, broke away from her side and made her way around the roller-rink to where I was and began to skate at my side. "There she is. Go to her" she said to me with her very encouraging smile. That was just the green light I needed. I hurriedly skated around the room and slowly made my way to her side. I moved up to her so as to not startle her and said to her: "I am not too steady on these wheels. Maybe we should hold hands so neither of us falls down." "That sounds like a good idea to me." she said. Neither of us came close to falling down that night. It was an evening of joy beyond my wildest imagination until Virginia said to me: "I came with a date tonight but he doesn't skate. He has been sitting on the sidelines watching us all evening. I will have to go home with him tonight but I will tell him that there will be no more dates for us anymore." When I heard those words my heart raced with the hope for many more skating moments in the future for the two of us. Maybe even some moments where I could skate backwards while looking into those beautiful brown eyes and watching that long pony-tail moving seductively from side to side. I have been skating in circles with her for the past 68 years. Ahh, summer camp is a wonderful thing. So is Vaseline in a jar!

It wouldn't be long before I would be heading north to Bible college in San Jose once again and Virginia would be remaining in the southern part of the state to attend another Christian college closer to her home. Just a few more days and my separation from Southern California and Virginia Anderson would once again define my social existence. Once again that same feeling of separation that had so often characterized much of my life would occur between me and someone I loved or at least between me and someone I was beginning to love. It would be a growing feeling between me and the person who would someday become my wife, or at least I hoped would turn out to be my wife. One evening before my departure north, Virginia and I were sitting together on the front row in a church service holding and sharing a church hymnal in our hands. Other than keeping each other from falling on the floor at a skating rink we had not touched each other in any amorous way to this point in our friendship. But in holding that hymnal together in our two hands our fingers were dangerously close to one another. I had the overwhelming feeling that no amount of sanctified holiness within either of us was going to keep our two fingers from amorously touching each other that night. I was right. First, there was an ever so light a touch (accidental?) between our two fingers beneath the cover of the church hymnal. First the touch and then the electricity! Then a slightly stronger touch of our two fingers and, wow, an even greater charge of electricity. All of this was followed by the partial loss of my ability to breathe very well or to sing any church music at all. Finally, there was the growing feeling that I might even faint dead away before the Almighty in this very holy place. All of this heavy emotion was flowing within me right in front of God and all those holy people who were engaged in thinking their collective spiritual thoughts together. Everyone in the room was doing that except me. There was only one thing I felt I could possibly do to not let this super-charged moment slip away from me forever. I took my finger and grabbed her sweet little complicit (?) finger and held on to it for dear life. That is exactly what I did that night and have been doing for the past 68 years. I do not remember the name of that church song we were singing that evening but I do remember the names of those two breathless individuals who were trying their best to somehow sing some of it. Later on that evening I gave her my letterman's sweater to wear that I had earned at Crater High School from engaging in track and basketball athletics. It was made quite clear to everyone by the passing of my athletic sweater to her that evening that we were now officially boyfriend and girlfriend. In the eyes of everyone we knew we were 'going steady' as they referred to it in those days. That sweater still hangs in my clothes closet today. It doesn't quite fit either one of us today as it once did, however, we still seem to fit one another just fine!

Following the next school year, when summer arrived, I was given the opportunity by the Air Force for an all-expenses paid trip to visit my parents in Germany where they lived because I was still considered to be their dependent. It had been two years since I had last seen both my parents and my three sisters since they had moved to Europe. Since the Air Force was willing to pay my way to see them it was an opportunity of a lifetime to see much of Europe at the same time as well. It had only been ten years since the Second World War had ended and much of Germany still lay in considerable ruins. This trip would provide me a great opportunity to see the German people up close and personal. I was excitedly looking forward to it. Virginia, however, had been persuaded by one of her girlfriends to break up with me while I was gone so she could be free to date others while I was away for those three months. My heart was broken by her decision to do that so I went to Germany with one eye on my new German friends and the other eye on the mental image of that beautiful pony-tail waving in the warm California sunshine and appealing to other young men my age who couldn't keep their eyes off of her. I couldn't help but wonder if she was holding the hands of someone I was sure couldn't skate nearly as well as I thought I could. I knew we were both planning to attend the same Christian seminary in Cincinnati, Ohio in the fall. "Perhaps we could start all over together again" I heard myself thinking out loud one day in Germany. Years later, after several courses in psychology, I learned that if feelings for another person are not continuously fed or nourished they tend to atrophy or diminish over time. I so hoped that such a thing would not happen to either one of us. It certainly didn't happen to me since I stirred those feelings of longing within me by writing her long, loving letters each day while we were separated from one another. Virginia did not do the same thing on her end and as a result of that her feelings for me became more confused and unclear. I couldn't help but wonder how I could help her clarify how she felt about me. I came home to the United States and to the Cincinnati Bible Seminary, my new school, with a new flat-top haircut (the current rage among young people in Europe) which certainly did not help my case with Virginia one little bit. Virginia hated that haircut and she clearly let me know how she felt. I hadn't given much thought to the fact that Virginia might not like it at all. I knew that Virginia had to make up her own mind about me and that trying to force her in my direction wouldn't help my cause at all. So, there seemed to be only one strategic action on my part that might help me. Her older sister, Pat, was also enrolled in the same school as Virginia and I were. So, I told Pat privately of an idea I had and wondered if she would work with me in carrying out a private plot I had to make things better between Virginia and me. I approached Pat and asked her: "Would you be willing to go out on a date with me?" Pat understood where I was coming from and thought that it might just be worth the effort on our part, albeit Pat thought it was a pretty sneaky strategy to make her sister a little jealous by her going out on a date with me. I agreed with her that it was a sneaky strategy indeed but that desperate situations sometimes called for desperate strategies. So, Pat and I went out on a non-romantic date together. Our date had the intended results. Virginia was quite angry and a little hurt with both Pat and me. We understood that fact and felt she had a right to feel that way. However, I explained to Virginia that after all it was she who broke up with me, not the other way around. The simple truth was that after that date with her older sister, Pat, Virginia quickly discovered that I mattered a great deal to her. That momentary connection with Pat brought about a fresh beginning for both Virginia and me in finding our way back to each other again. The trees were changing their green leaves to red, yellow, and orange in Ohio in that beautiful moment in October when Virginia and I found our way back to each other one more time. It was a moment of beautiful change in the land around us and also inside both Ginny and me too. Thank God for that and thank God for Pat as well.

Several months later I made a secret arrangement to borrow a friend's car so I could arrange for a very special date with Virginia. I had been setting aside several dollars each week to purchase an engagement ring for her at a jewelry store near the seminary and I wanted to drive her to a very romantic place in Cincinnati to give that ring to her. But first I wanted to telephone her father in Long Beach to formally ask him for her daughter's hand in marriage. That seemed like the time-honored traditional thing for me to do. I was told by Mrs. Anderson that Virginia's father would be in an important meeting on the night I had intended to call him but that he would step out of the meeting when he received word that I was on the phone ready to talk to him. I went downtown to find an outdoor telephone booth to make the call from and I put a large pile of nickels and dimes on the little shelf inside the phone booth to use to make the long-distance call. The very moment I got Mr. Anderson on the other end of the call a long string of very large trucks passed by my phone booth. I had made the terrible mistake of selecting a phone booth located on the corner of one of the city's busiest intersections. Every truck would have to noisily shift gears to slow down as it turned that corner next to my selected phone booth. I could hear nothing on my end of the telephone line as they turned the corner next to me and the phone booth. I kept saying to Mr. Anderson: "Can you speak up, sir. I cannot hear you." This was repeated several times and my pile of coins was quickly disappearing in front of me. I was desperate and didn't know what I was going to do if I ran out of money and could not complete my call. Miraculously, the string of noisy trucks finally came to an end and I heard

Mr. Anderson's clear voice finally coming through my telephone's receiver with these words: "Larry I would be most happy to have you as my son-in-law. Just love her as much as we have all loved her these many years and we will be very happy for you to have her as your wife." "There certainly is a God!" I couldn't help but think to myself as I picked up the two nickels I had left on the little shelf in front of me. "Just think" I remember saying to myself "Reuben Anderson is soon going to be my father-in-law!"

We had a curfew time set at 11:00 p.m. at the Seminary for all the females on campus. The administrative staff believed that if they could get all the girls in their rooms by 11:00 p.m. that all the guys would probably go to their rooms about the same time as well. So, I quickly realized that I had to borrow my friend's car, pick up Virginia for our short date, and then find my way to that romantic location to give her the engagement ring I had in a beautiful ring box. And, of course, I had to do all of this within the time limit to meet the curfew requirement for females on campus. The romantic location I had in mind was called Echo Park. All the young people I knew called it 'Necko Park', the place where young lovers could go to romantically make out on their dates. The problem was I couldn't find where the park was located since it was very dark outside. I realized that I was beginning to drive too fast and a bit too recklessly because I was worried that I wouldn't be able to give her the ring at all because I was running out of the time required to meet the curfew deadline. Virginia knew I was looking for Echo Park and she just assumed that I was driving fast because I wanted to find a romantic spot where we could hug and kiss for a while. I tried to tell her that that was not my intent without disclosing to her just why I was in such a hurry to find that romantic location. I was just about to tell her that I was simply wanting to give her an engagement ring but I didn't want the evening to end in such an anti-climatic way. Once again, I was favored with divine intervention when the entrance to the park miraculously opened up before me. I raced to the very top of the hill overlooking the city of Cincinnati and all its beautiful lights below. I turned the car's engine off and within a couple of seconds I pulled the ring-box out of my jacket pocket, opened it, recited the short engagement speech I had previously rehearsed, kissed her quickly, and started the car's engine telling her at the same time that we had to hurry back to the campus in time to meet the curfew deadline! It was probably the shortest proposal on record but it has held firmly for almost seven decades. Two years later, with my new flat-top haircut fully grown out to its old hair style once again, Virginia and I got married!

The seminary I attended was theologically quite a conservative school. I shared a big part of my father's very inquiring and curious mind. Dad was never afraid to question the deeply-held social or philosophical ideas that he or other people believed. I found myself quite often asking my professors similar 'why' or 'why not' questions. I often heard, in my head, the voice of my father asking about intellectual issues that did not seem to make any sense to him. This inclination of mine sometimes caused some contentious discussions in our classes at school. Frequently some of my friends would tell me that they did not feel they could be friends with me any longer because of some of the unacceptable or questionable views I seemed to hold. Those, of course, were hurtful sentiments for me to hear from them. I had always held to the idea that honest intellectual inquiries should never stand in the way of one's friendship and fondness toward others. I was to later learn in seminary that it was very rare for friendships to successfully survive intellectual disagreements with one another. I often invited older and more mature scholars into my home for dinner and discussions on subjects that would have been out of favor with some of the views held by either the students or faculty members on our conservative campus. I would invite other like-minded friends of mine to share in these lively discussions on various controversial issues. The word of these meetings, of course, would circulate on campus concerning these somewhat 'unorthodox' scholars I invited into our home and I began to be perceived by some on campus as becoming a part of a less-than-acceptable religious community that existed beyond the boundaries of our seminary. In spite of these moments of intellectual discomfort on campus I thoroughly loved the sometimes rough-and-tumble intellectual atmosphere during those wonderful seminary years.

I excelled in the academic area of school earning an almost straight-A scorecard in all of my courses throughout my four years in college. In those four college years I received one B and one B+ and all the rest were A's in my classes. One day at school, just before graduation, the President of the seminary called me into his office because he wanted to have a talk with me. I had no idea what was on his mind so I somewhat tentatively entered his office and sat down in front of his desk. "Was he going to give me a dressing down because of some of those controversial meetings I had been holding in my home?" I thought to myself. He quickly thanked me for coming to see him and he began to speak these words to me: "We were very happy when you transferred to our school from the San Jose Bible College where you had served with considerable academic distinction for two years with a straight-A average. You have served the past two years at our school with almost the very same average. Normally, with that outstanding scholarly record you would be given the highest academic award among all our graduating seniors -- the Valedictorian Award -- at the final graduation ceremony. However, regrettably Larry, we cannot do that because we have a rule at our school that states that a person has to attend at least three years here in order for that award to be given." I stood and quietly, but very sadly, left his office. I have learned in life that official rules often don't make a person feel a whole lot better when it is discovered that they are sometimes used to justify a course of behavior that could be seen as inherently unfair. I came to realize that other awards would perhaps come to me in later years. However, this award apparently had been more anticipated by me than I had fully understood or admitted in my heart that it was. The award's loss would likely take a little more time and maturity on my part to more fully understand and process. I later came to understand that while people and rules could certainly take this desired award away from me they could never remove all that treasured knowledge and joy those lettered-grades brought to me. My visit to the President's office was a lot like that previous visit with Mr. Applebury in his office three years earlier. I would undoubtedly more fully understand the deeper truth or meaning of those two painful meetings in my life when I was older and wiser. At least I hoped so. These reflections about my earlier painful experiences in life didn't erase the pain of those earlier moments but they did serve as a bridge to help me get past the kind of pain that can sometimes end up creating a self-defeating path of vengeful responses in life when pain darkens one's pathway.

13

My new Indiana home.

A few months later I took the biggest step in my ministerial career to date. I had been wanting to find a small church to minister to somewhere in the surrounding states of Indiana, Kentucky, or Ohio while I was engaged in the final months of my seminary schooling. Some of the students at the seminary, where I was attending, had found local congregations they served as 'preaching points' for them on Sundays. A preaching point was a church to which the ministerial student would travel to serve on the weekends. Serving the church usually involved visiting the church members in their homes, organizing and spending time with the young people in the church and, most importantly for both the seminary student as well as the congregation, the student would preach at the morning worship service as well as the evening worship service if the church had an evening service scheduled. Serving a local congregation was a very busy and demanding time for these young seminary students on the weekends because the weekends were the specific times when the young seminarians would travel to those churches and serve them in those challenging and life-maturing ways. These preaching points were invaluable training experiences for the young minister because no church would hire them after graduation if they had not had previous clergy experience in a local congregational setting. Most of these young men and I say 'men' because in those days – the 1950's – no women were allowed to preach in most churches at that time. These young seminarians were carrying a full load of academic studies during the week. Most of them also had part-time jobs in the afternoons and evenings after their morning classes were completed each day. Tuition had to be paid for and rent and food costs had to be taken care of as well. Most of these seminarians would return from their weekend preaching points to their home at the seminary late Sunday evenings to continue studying late into the evening hours to make preparation for their seminary classes early Monday morning. I was fortunate to obtain a preaching point in my third year of college. I was thrilled to obtain such a ministerial assignment. It made me feel that I finally had arrived in my quest to be a full-fledged minister in service for God. It was a great feeling to finally become an active, serving, minister, not just a student studying for the ministry. But I quickly learned that I was not going to be a full-time minister. I was only going to be a half-time minister. The church to which I was being invited to preach was called the Blue Lick Christian Church located in the small farming community of Henryville, Indiana. The church had approximately 100 people who attended regularly on Sunday mornings for Sunday School classes and twice a month it would hold worship services where the minister would preach. We also had evening worship services as well on those two Sundays which meant that I would have to preach twice on those Sundays, both morning and evening. That is why we referred to churches like that as 'half-time' churches. They only had worship services twice a month which included a sermon and holy communion. The church was located 125 miles from the seminary in Cincinnati, Ohio. The 250-

mile round trip to my preaching point was a considerable challenge for me considering I did not have an automobile with which to make the trip. So, each week I had to either catch a ride with a friend who would be making his trip to his preaching point nearby or sometimes I would be lucky enough to borrow a car from one of my friends for the weekend. Most often, however, I would catch a ride to my church on a Greyhound bus. The Blue Lick Christian Church to which I was called was almost 100 years old and as far as anyone could remember they had always been a half-time church. That is what I was signed up for. I was employed to preach twice a month (both Sunday mornings and Sunday evenings) and to develop educational programs for the young people on Saturdays. I was paid $35 dollars a weekend for my efforts. The cost of the Greyhound bus ride took one-third of what I was paid on the Sundays I visited the church. The church offering was counted after the worship service was completed on Sunday mornings and one-dollar bills were counted out into my hand at the front door by the church treasurer. No one seemed to have ever put more money in the offering plates than a one-dollar bill. Sometimes several dollars of my agreed-upon financial salary was given to me in various denominations of coins. When the Sunday offering did not quite cover my agreed-upon amount the congregation had promised to pay me, the farmers would chip in and pay me the rest of my salary in chickens, eggs, and vegetables from their own farms. I found the entire process a little embarrassing as I stood at the door of the church with my hand extended out in front of me never quite knowing what my hand would end up being filled with. It was also a little uncomfortable having to get on the Greyhound bus on Sunday night loaded down with bags of chickens, eggs and vegetables along with my suitcase and Bible.

A few months after arriving at the church as their new minister I presented to the congregation the idea of becoming a full-time church. What that would mean was that instead of the congregation meeting only two times a month for holy communion and preaching they would have my presence to lead them in church worship services each Sunday of the month. They said to me that for 100 years they had always been a half-time church and had never considered becoming a full-time church. I quickly learned that two of their favorite expressions were: "We've <u>never</u> done things like that" or "We've <u>always</u> done things like this." I urged them to think about my proposal and talk it over among themselves and we would speak about it at another time. The people began to gradually warm up to the idea. Finally, someone said the actual words out loud that many of them had been thinking in their hearts: "Well, why not give it a try!" So, that is exactly what we did. For the first time in 100 years the Blue Lick Christian Church would become a full-time church! There would be a preacher in the pulpit every Sunday morning and every Sunday evening! We would also have a communion service every Sunday as well.

Within the following year Virginia and I got married. She had been attending my preaching point with me every Sunday for some time and the people loved her. She added so much to the growing success of my ministry. Since I paid her way on the bus it dawned on me that I was working the entire weekend for ten dollars. It was clear that I certainly was not doing this work for the money! Attendance was growing and the influence of a woman's presence in the work was clearly noticeable and impactful. I was about to finish my education at the seminary and the congregation had expected that I would move on to a larger church as all of the seminary ministers they had hired prior to me had done before. Virginia had become pregnant in my last year at school and we were not anxious to move on to some other church location we did not know. We loved the people in Henryville and they loved us. Furthermore, they had adjusted extremely well to moving from part-time status to full-time status as a church and we felt that it was time for them to consider hiring, for the first time in 100 years, a full-time minister who would actually live within their own church location and would spiritually guide the church during the week and not just on the weekends alone. "How much money would you need per week if you moved here?" they asked us. We had done some figuring and came to the conclusion that if we received $65 dollars a week we could make ends meet (I couldn't help but remember my mother saying years earlier to us children: "it's all about 'making ends meet' in this life!"). "That is almost double what we have been paying you before" one of the leaders said to us. "How do you suggest we come up with the added amount?" he asked me. I had come to know these people pretty well over the past two years and felt their anguish in considering our new financial proposition to them. They loved us, to be sure, but the financial challenge seemed formidable from their perspective. I suggested that they tell the congregation the following Sunday morning about what the leaders of the church were considering. I told the leaders to tell the people to go home and pray about it and decide privately within their own family how much each person or family could afford to contribute each Sunday in order to have their own minister living within their community and serving full-time in their midst. Within the next couple of weeks the people in the congregation were told that on the following Sunday each person in attendance would be asked to write on a piece of un-signed paper an amount they would be willing to contribute each week to have the Keene's permanently move into their community as their full-time minister. The next Sunday we all gathered at church and those financial commitments by the members of the church were written on small pieces of paper and they were collected and counted following the morning worship service. It was agreed by the church that if the amount pledged by the membership met or exceeded $65 dollars a week we would be hired as their full-time minister. Needless to say, on the day when the tabulations were to be made the excitement and tension were running quite high. Virginia and I could hardly breathe as the process was played out in front of all of us. We so wanted to come and live and work with these dear people. Finally, the tabulations were completed. Two volunteers from the congregation did the counting. Nickels, dimes, quarters, and dollar weekly commitments were made by the church members. There was even one five-dollar weekly commitment made by one member. These sums were added up and recorded. You could hear a pin drop in that little country church that Sunday morning. Finally, the counting was finished. The total pledged for the new minister's weekly salary was: $65.75! We were 75 cents above the goal we had set for ourselves for coming to the church full-time. But, we were above the line and that was what counted! Everyone burst forth with enthusiastic applause. The Keene's were coming to Henryville, Indiana! We all cried. Within a few months of that glorious day the congregation was receiving over $400 dollars in our morning offering, <u>each</u> Sunday. The Lord mightily blessed all of us in the church as we shared with one another in the ministry at this wonderful country church. Our first child, Lance, was born while we were there and we were so excited to share him with all those wonderful people. We are still friends and communicate with some of these people to this very day, sixty five years later. In fact, I was invited back a few years ago to preach at their 150th anniversary as a congregation. Virginia and I were there with them on their 100th anniversary and with them once again 50 years later. Virginia was asked to sing once more for them as she often did when we were with them. They have built, in the years following our time with them, an entirely new sanctuary and fellowship hall on their present site and have also built a youth recreation center on a new property they had purchased a short distance from their original church property. For 65 years they have continued to employ a full-time minister in residence at their church. That was a pivotal time in the life of that congregation and Virginia and I feel humbled that we were there to share in the excitement and joy of those first visionary steps the church took in those early days in our Christian ministry.

Just before Virginia and I moved back to California to continue my education there, I performed my very first wedding for our friends Bill and Vada Dietrich who had been active as leaders in the church even though they were barely out of high school when we came to Henryville. They were our age and we were very close to one another as friends. Their wedding was planned for the summer and Indiana summers were quite hot and humid. When the Elders of the church heard of the upcoming wedding and that Bill and Vada wanted me to perform their wedding they called me in for a private meeting with them. I was puzzled as to the purpose of the meeting so I asked them why they wanted to talk to me. They said that they were insisting that I be officially ordained as a minister before I performed the wedding so I would have legal status with the State of Indiana to perform weddings as a minister. It seems that a previous minister of theirs had done a wedding at their church and he had not been previously ordained as a minister to do so and that the wedding had to be nullified and done all over again after he had become officially ordained to do weddings. There was great embarrassment and anger in the congregation over the entire matter so the Elders were not going to go through that experience again. So, on with the shotgun ordination we went in a hurry so we could make further plans for the wedding. On the day of their wedding the church was packed. All the windows were open for increased ventilation and to allow the overflow audience to peek in the windows as they listened from the outside. I had rehearsed my wedding ceremony out loud for hours and hours beforehand. Virginia also knew the words of my ceremony by heart because of the numerous times she had heard me recite it in her presence. However, when I got in front of the congregation that night I looked out into that sea of faces in front of me and my nervousness got the best of me as this was the very first wedding I had ever performed (I have done over 8,000 weddings since and I am no longer nervous doing weddings). I was so nervous that I completely forgot every single word I had memorized and practiced for hours to deliver. I knew I had to say something. I was the minister after all, so for about ten minutes I just faked it. I wandered from one statement about love I had ever heard before thinking that if I would continue talking about the subject of love that I would perhaps accidentally stumble on to some phrase or statement I had previously written and memorized. I reasoned that then I could successfully transition to the completion of my wedding ceremony. I could see that Virginia was dying with agony for me while sitting in the congregation. She knew where I should be going in my memorized ceremony and she also knew I wasn't anywhere close to getting where I needed to be. That frightening ministerial moment of mine reminds me of a similar scene in a movie I saw many years later entitled: "Three weddings and a funeral." In the movie a young minister was doing his very first wedding ceremony. The panic he felt in performing that holy ministerial function for the first time was exactly what I was feeling on that hot summer afternoon in Indiana in 1958. Finally, after fumbling around in the dark for several minutes in that packed, very humid church building, I finally said something that seemed to fit into the script that I had previously memorized and so I followed that line of thinking to where I needed to be in my wedding ceremony. Everything began to go quite well for me in the wedding service until I said to the groom: "Do you take this <u>man</u> to be your lawfully wedded <u>wife</u>?" Everyone in the church giggled and I was lost once again in the ceremonial weeds. In that moment I wanted to be a plumber not a minister. My clothes were soaked with perspiration and it was not from the summer heat. It was from my fright and inexperience. I somehow made it through to the completion of Bill and Vada's wedding service. The two of them were finally successfully married on that warm summer day in Indiana and they have been among our closest of friends for the past 59 years. We have traveled across the country to go on vacations together and have stayed in their beautiful home Bill built with his own hands in the first year of their marriage. Vada died recently just short of their 60th wedding anniversary. True to his skill as a carpenter, Bill built the beautiful casket his wife Vada was buried in. It was without a doubt their love for one another that enabled their marriage to endure through those many years, not the skill of the clergyman who clumsily performed their wedding a long time ago!

14

My new California home.

Following our big move to Indiana, Virginia gave birth to our first child. Lance was born in the city of Cincinnati (as was his mother several years earlier) and in the city where my seminary education was completed as well. We went to the Hoosier state not only with the challenge of growing and expanding our new ministry with the Blue Lick Christian Church but with the challenge of growing our new child as well. I was very excited about bringing several boxes of religious books from Cincinnati to Indiana for my new library in my church office. One non-theological book, however, also found its way into our family library. It was a small book written by a man named Dr. Spock entitled: **Baby and Child Care**. Virginia and I used that marvelous book to guide us through the raising of all five of our children. The book was well-worn by the time Kathryn, our last child, was born. The pages were falling out of it and the book was being held together by a large rubber band. We could have replaced it for a new one but we felt that it had certain magical and curative powers embedded in it that guaranteed we would have good luck with each succeeding child so we kept the book and the big rubber band as well!

When Lance had reached his first birthday in Indiana we decided it was time for us to return to California to continue my education at Pepperdine University in Los Angeles. The two and a half years we spent ministering in Indiana were very rewarding ones for us and convinced us that being an ordained minister and serving on behalf of good church people was an inspired and blessed choice on our part. It also became increasingly clear to me that being educationally prepared to minister to increasingly sophisticated parishioners in this day and age would require further study and preparation on my part. So, we packed up our 1949 Chevrolet sedan with Virginia, Lance, and me and we headed west to Pepperdine University in Los Angeles.

Coming back to California also meant coming back to Virginia's five siblings and mother and father as well. Lance was the first grandchild for Virginia's parents. They were ecstatic with our move west. An additional advantage for me in making this move was being closer to Virginia's father, Reuben. Reuben Anderson was one of the most-respected ministers in the United States. He ministered to a congregation that had over 3000 members (the largest Christian Church west of the Mississippi River at that time). I stood in awe of this humble and caring minister. Being able to draw upon his wisdom and experience was a treasure I wanted to explore and to more fully appreciate up close. In the early years of my ministry I was often introduced as: Reuben Anderson's son-in-law or a little later as Virginia Anderson's husband. Still, later on I was quite often introduced as: Lance's father. I have learned that it sometimes takes a great deal of time before some of us are introduced for who he or she actually is on his or her own terms. For some of us it takes longer than others to accomplish this. I was one of those people who had to be more patient until that time came to him.

Upon reaching Southern California I was quickly interviewed and hired to become the associate minister to one of the very large and successful churches in Inglewood, California. One Sunday after I had been at the church for two years, the Senior Minister was away on vacation and I was in the pulpit preaching the morning sermon. There was a visiting couple in the congregation I did not recognize. They remained behind after the worship service had ended to talk with me. They had just arrived in the United States on their own vacation from Maracaibo, Venezuela. They explained to me that they were delegated by their local congregation to find a minister for their newly-established congregation in that far-away Venezuelan city. All of the members of their church had come from different Christian denominations and they were all employed in some part of the oil industry located in Maracaibo. Most of the people in their church were relatively young and were willing to take a chance at working overseas since the financial remuneration for doing so was very good. In short, they were looking for a young minister who was willing to take a chance at ministering to their fledgling congregation. They were willing to pay me $1000 per month if I would come to be their very first minister in residence. That was about three times a greater ministerial salary than I had ever received before. I told them that I would need a little time to think that offer over but that I was not just going to turn the offer down. The excitement of going overseas to minister to Americans there really appealed to Virginia and me. It was not nearly so appealing to Virginia's family, however. The significant geographic separation from them was a big part of their unwillingness to encourage us to leave California. The implicit danger of living in a strange country that none of us knew very much about was an additional factor in their negative feelings about us leaving the safety of our country as well as leaving Virginia's family behind. We definitely felt a huge push-back from them. It was not until many years later when our own children contemplated moving away from us with their little children (our grandchildren) could we more fully understand how Virginia's parents felt in that moment when we approached them about moving several thousand miles away with our little children (their grandchildren).

However, in spite of our parents' reluctance about our leaving, we decided to go to Venezuela to begin a new ministry in this far-off country. On the day of our departure, we hurriedly arrived at the Los Angeles International Airport with the grandparents running after us carrying our two little children in their arms. We had mistaken the departure time for the airplane that was going to take us to Venezuela. The gate attendants were holding the airplane for us with its propellers already turning, making ready for its departure until we got on board. We flew from Los Angeles to Havana, Cuba and landed there before we continued on to Maracaibo, Venezuela. We learned a little later that our airplane was the very last American airplane that was to land in Cuba before they finally closed all flights to and from Cuba because of their recent national revolution. Those airplane flights have been closed even until this very day. Because of our hurried departure from the Los Angeles air terminal, we were not able to acquire the appropriate boarding card that would have allowed us to de-plane from the airplane and go into the air-terminal in Havana for a few minutes with the other passengers. All the other passengers de-planed for the short lay-over in Cuba and Virginia and I and the children were left on the airplane, all alone. We looked out the windows and saw that the airplane was surrounded by at least 25 soldiers in their green army uniforms with each one of them holding a machine gun in their arms guarding our plane. We were filled with fear. Finally, after about an hour's wait, all of the other passengers came back to the plane and our KLM Airline passenger plane started its engines once again and we flew away – the last American passenger plane to do so from Cuba, ever. It was a story we left unshared with the Anderson family until we returned home from Venezuela three years later.

For three years we happily ministered to this American, English-speaking congregation. It was the first congregation our denomination, the

Christian Church (Disciples of Christ), had ever established in the entire country of Venezuela. While we were there for those three years our third son, Bryan, was born, joining Lance and Kenneth before him. Interestingly, the doctor who delivered our new son also delivered, in that very same week, the very first male sextuplets ever born in Venezuela. I was so glad that the stork sent those six baby boys to that other set of parents instead of to us that week! Our new son was given Venezuelan citizenship along with his United States citizenship until he reached the age of eighteen. At that time he had to choose which citizenship he would retain for the rest of his life. He is, today, living in Oceanside, California as a proud American citizen (with Venezuelan roots!).

Venezuela, at the time was a thriving, pro-American country. While their democratic system of government was only about three years old at that time, the people were still struggling with the notion of what it meant to be a democratic country, free from tyranny and dictatorship which characterized the governments of so many other South-American countries at the time. For instance, the idea or notion of being a free democracy where people could do the many things they had previously not been allowed to do, caused some people while driving their automobiles to disregard or ignore the stop signs at the street corners (all, of course, in the name of their newly-discovered freedom). This notion resulted in many intersections being greatly clogged with people who would not yield their way to others because they were now 'free'. Someone there once said to me, in describing the Venezuelans' experience with freedom and democracy: "Venezuelans' have simply moved too quickly from the burro to the automobile."

After three very rewarding years of ministry with our American friends and our newly-found Venezuelan friends, we decided to return to America to continue the graduate education that I had previously put on hold in order to accept the wonderful challenge of organizing and ministering to this new church. We moved once more to Southern California where all of Virginia's family still lived and were anxiously waiting for us to return. We had been in conversation with one of the most successful Christian Churches in all of Southern California. The Crenshaw Christian Church was also located in Inglewood as the previous congregation we had served was. It had 1000 members and they wanted me to come as their Associate Minister. The minister had been in his position for over 30 years. While he had strong segregationist beliefs that led him to not allow African-American people to obtain membership in his congregation, I felt that I could be a good influence in moderating and, in time, bringing about a change in that point of view in the church. I shared with him how my views were different than his but that I would respect his point of view and not create dissension within the church on this matter. In time, I felt feelings would change and I would be able to serve as a transitional figure in the church's growth on this issue. The Senior Minister felt that this response of mine was very fair on my part and so he decided to take a chance on me, so I was hired. For two years we ministered amicably and effectively to this wonderful congregation. In 1965 Dr. Appelgate, the Senior Minister, decided to retire. I was 27 years old at the time. The ruling elders were faced with the task of replacing Dr. Appelgate by finding a new minister for this large and well-educated congregation. They were impressed by the fact that I was about to finish my Master's degree at Pepperdine University and would soon be starting my Doctoral degree program at the University of Southern California. "Let's take a chance on this young man," one of the Elders said in the Elders' meeting. And, that is just what they did. They took a chance on me and I took a chance on them as well.

Our little family moved into married-student housing on the Pepperdine University campus. Those two-room apartments were refurbished army barracks that had been salvaged after the Second World War and put into use for married students at the school. There was: one bedroom where the three boys slept on triple bunk-beds, one very small bathroom, and one kitchen-living room area where our front-room davenport made into a bed each evening for Virginia and me. It was very small and very cozy and very inexpensive. I had painted the floor with a glossy dark brown paint and Virginia had made beautiful curtains for the windows. Virginia said: "It's a little like putting lipstick on an old lady. It isn't perfect but it is an improvement." We made $300 per month in salary from the church and the monthly rent for our apartment was $65 a month. We were thrilled with the arrangement. With the additional baby-sitting money Virginia earned each month we were able to 'make ends meet' as my mother used to say. I felt that God blessed us in so many numerous ways through our post-war experiences in America. I not only got my father back safely from the big war but we were also provided these crude army barracks for my growing family to live in as well. It was not lost on us that as we went to sleep each night in these made-over Army barracks, the very same kind of barracks my father also went to sleep in each night when he was in the army. In his wildest imagination I do not think my father could have ever entertained the thought that when he laid his head down to sleep in his army bunk at night that one day his little grandchildren would also lay their heads down to fall asleep in the very same kind of dwelling he fell asleep in at night. Life will sometimes really make us smile in surprising ways for sure.

15

Learning to wear two hats in my growing home.

I received my Master's degree in sociology in 1965 from Pepperdine University in Los Angeles. I immediately began teaching in their sociology department upon the completion of my graduate degree. I was hired at the rank of Instructor 1. The ranking system for those teaching at Pepperdine involved 13 different ranks from the lowest rank to the highest rank. They were as follows:

    Instructor 1
    Instructor 2
    Instructor 3

Assistant Professor 1

Assistant Professor 2

Assistant Professor 3

Associate Professor 1

Associate Professor 2

Associate Professor 3

Professor 1

Professor 2

Professor 3

Professor Emeritus

In the 40 years I taught at Pepperdine I went through all of these 13 levels of instruction from the lowest to the highest rank. My tenure at the university, when I retired from teaching there, was also longer than any other professor who had ever taught there before. The only ranking higher than the rank of full professor 3 was the title:

Professor Emeritus. It was an honorary title given for outstanding scholarly achievement and distinguished teaching performance at the time of one's retirement. Of the several thousand professors who had been employed by Pepperdine since its beginning in 1937, only a small handful of professors had received that honorary distinction from the school. I was fortunate to have been one of those professors. Every year one professor in the entire faculty was selected by the members of the student body to be the 'Outstanding teacher of the year.' I had received that honor a dozen times (more times than had any other teacher in the history of the school). At the annual student assembly, where the winner of the award was announced, I began feeling that I did not want to any longer attend the assembly program because of my growing embarrassment at my being introduced once again as the winner of that award. I could not help feeling some sense of jealousy from some of the professors for having been bypassed by the students for this wonderful honor. I also have to admit, as I am writing these words, of having some embarrassment at mentioning these honors at all in this autobiography but Virginia reminded me many times to just: "Tell your story . . . <u>all</u> of it!" So, that's what I will do. I received, of course, many other scholarly and teaching awards from Pepperdine but the professor emeritus award stands out as my most personally satisfying accomplishment during my 40 years of teaching at my beloved alma mater.

In my earliest days of teaching at Pepperdine the salary was very minimal at those lower ranks of teaching. I begged the school to give me more classes to teach so I could earn more over-time money to support my family.

There were times when I was actually carrying a double teaching load (32 total units of classwork) at school. That had never happened at the university before but it had become necessary for me to earn more money because of the expanding size of our family. Because of the added preparation time this teaching load required of me I would arrive at school sometimes as early as 3:00 o'clock in the morning and I would use one of my credit cards to slip through the locked doors at the school in order to get into my office to study for the classes I would have to teach that day. The janitors were amused that this young minister-professor would be so bold as to break into the school's locked doors in order to have a quiet place to study. This also gave me an opportunity to have a cup of hot coffee with the janitors who worked all night to clean the classrooms for the students who would arrive there for their 8:00 A.M. classes. I would use these early hours to also study for the graduate classes I was taking at the same time for my doctoral degree at the University of Southern California. I only got about three hours of sleep each night in those days and I often wondered at the time just how many years off my life were being lost by this very difficult work schedule of mine.

I tried to expose my students to more than just their acquaintance with the wonderful world of sociological and anthropological literature that was available to them through my teaching. As important and beneficial as that literature was to their learning I also tried to personally immerse them in the surrounding neighborhood culture of the many diverse kinds of people who lived near our university in those days. Many of my students came from Caucasian backgrounds of economic privilege and I wanted them to deepen their understanding of the diverse richness of the cultures that existed in our area of Southern California. Many of the major assignments they were given in my courses required them to participate for several weeks in social settings very different from the ones they experienced in growing up in their own family environs previous to their coming to college in California. Following these assigned participation studies the students would be required to report their social immersion experiences with their sociology or anthropology class and to state in sociological or anthropological language what they saw and what they came to understand and what they emotionally felt from their social exposure to these new cultural experiences. Because of these community investigations by my students, many of them went on to graduate schools of education to become professors in the field of sociology or anthropology. Several of my innovative classes were written up and described in *Time Magazine* and other national publications as examples of imaginative college instruction in today's universities. I always thought, as many dedicated teachers told me they did as well, that I learned as much if not more than my students did in the process of being a teacher. And to think the school paid me to do it. I probably would have gladly done it for free if the truth were really known. But, unfortunately, my little children loved to eat so money came to be one of my important considerations in my employment as a teacher!

Teaching at Pepperdine was only one of the two work hats I wore during that exciting time living in the mid-sixties. The other hat I wore was that of being the Senior Minister at the

Crenshaw Christian Church in Inglewood, California. Because of these two hats I wore I was selected to be included in the <u>Outstanding Young Men In America</u> annual edition. It was quite an honor, to be sure, but I always felt too shy to mention it to anyone so I just kept it to myself until I am now mentioning it for the very first time to the readers of this personal document.

Shortly after I was selected to be the Senior Minister of this large church, the city of Los Angeles was violently engulfed in the terrifying Watt's Riot which set South-Central Los Angeles ablaze with fire. There was rioting, and killing and wholesale destruction in that part of the city for several days. All of America saw the rioting played out on television each day as the devastation that was taking place on the city streets of Los Angeles was being laid out in full detail before our very eyes. Our church building was located very near to the center of all of that rioting activity. One of our church members, a policeman, was killed in that terrible mayhem. The community of Watts, where much of the violence was taking place, was made up of mostly African-American families. The church member of ours who was killed was a very progressive white policeman who supported the struggle that African-American people were having in obtaining justice and equity in our society. The policeman's partner, a white man, found himself struggling in a hand-to-hand fight with a black person who was looting a building during the riot. The gun the man was carrying went off during the struggle and killed our church member who was not involved in that struggle at all. Our church member was only one of a very few who was killed during the rioting and it seemed so sad to me that the very person who was so much in favor of civil rights for all people, and especially for black people, would have to die in such an unfortunate way. I remember leading the procession for the policeman's funeral which included over 1000 policemen from all over the state of California. The funeral was televised for all the nation to see on the evening news. It was a frightening beginning to my ministry in Southern California. I had to mature pretty quickly in my new ministerial position. From breaking into my university at 3:00 o'clock in the morning and studying for my classes, to checking the purses for guns and other weapons of the frightened elderly ladies in our church on Sunday mornings (some of which were actually packing guns in their purses), I quickly learned that the old rules which had guided how clergyman should perform their duties in those turbulent times had to be reconsidered and rewritten. I began to see that there were no clear blueprints for where and how my ministry was going to direct me as I plunged eagerly into my church-parish work. I have to admit that at the time I felt I was flying a little blind in knowing how I should lead in matters such as: racial equality, women's role in society and in the church, rights for homosexual people in society and, of course, their role in the church as well. I was feeling my way forward in my new ministry as if I was being guided by braille in so many of my decisions. With one foot in the classroom, and the other foot in the pulpit – the wearing of two hats if you will – I pushed my way forward, with God's help for sure, to a future place whose location was not at all clear to me at the time!

Our little family spent eight wonderful years at the Crenshaw Christian Church. Our three boys were now big boys by their own definition. The Crenshaw church in all its 60-year history had never had a minister with a girl-child in it. We were about to celebrate our 60th anniversary at our church and we had planned to make it a big event. Virginia was expecting our fourth child and I said to Virginia as we approached that big day: "If you can possibly help it (and, of course, she couldn't) please don't give birth to our new child on the night before the big event!" On the very night before the church's 60th anniversary, Virginia went into labor and gave the church a gift of a beautiful little girl (did I say she had dimples?). I had spent the entire night before our big celebration at the hospital waiting for the delivery of baby Nancy to take place. The mayor was to be at the church the following morning. All the major politicians in our city and a significant number of church dignitaries throughout southern California were also to be there. I had to secretly pay a bribe to our three sons by giving each of them one dollar if they kept the secret about whether they had a new baby brother or a new baby sister. I wanted to hold the church in suspense until the very end of the worship service when I would make the long-awaited-for announcement of baby Nancy's arrival. The boys wanted that money badly so their secret to not tell anyone the truth was safely secured. Finally, I stood before those 1000 people in attendance and said these words: "Our congregation has been waiting patiently for 60 years to hear these words . . . ." Before they heard the rest of my sentence all the people stood in unison and started applauding. They knew that the rest of the sentence would follow with something like this: ". . . a baby girl has finally been born to the ministry of the Crenshaw Christian Church." Everyone was so happy. I, on the other hand, who had been sleep-deprived the night before, was simply exhausted and ready to go home to bed for a well-deserved nap!

16

My two new Valley homes.

One of the great ministers in our denomination was an 87 year-old man named John Wells. He ministered to a very small congregation in the San Fernando Valley called The Little Brown Church in the Valley. In 1940 he built that small church building with his own hands. He posted a sign at the edge of the street in front of the proposed church site which said: "I am building a church for our community. Anyone wishing to give me a hand in doing this would be welcome to help me accomplish this. Just bring a hammer or saw with you and join me in this effort." Dozens of people stopped by each day to help him build the little church of his dreams. The total cost of building that entire structure in those days was $600. Two of the outstanding features of this little church was that the <u>l</u>ights inside the chapel would remain <u>on</u> all night, every night, throughout the year and the front door would remain <u>locked</u> <u>open</u> all night as well. In this way the church would always be available for prayer to people from all religious backgrounds whenever they felt the need for it. This policy was still in force in 1971 when I joined Brother Wells (as he liked to be called) as his associate. That policy is still in force to this day, 82 years later. Being hired by this wonderful small congregation was so very helpful to me as I was pursuing my doctoral studies at the time. Assisting in this new ministry proved to be an ideal arrangement for me as I was still teaching full-time at Pepperdine University and the lightened work-load at the church was an enormous help in fulfilling my teaching responsibilities as well as completing my studies. John Wells would preach on one Sunday at the church and I would preach the following Sunday. The church people liked it as well because it gave them a nice variety of sermonic styles to listen to from the pulpit week by week. I am not sure I would have ever been able to complete my studies for my degree if it had not been for this most generous offer from Brother Wells to assist him in this somewhat limited way.

Those next five years at The Little Brown Church were deeply rewarding ones for our family and me. Ministering to a small congregation with less demands on my time was so important in the raising of our young family. Raising teenagers is challenging at its best but raising them in the context of a small congregation where every adult was also a surrogate parent assisting Virginia and me in this task, was an enormous blessing to us as well. In 1976 Brother Wells died suddenly, at the age of 88, of a burst aneurysm in his abdomen. Taking over the entire ministerial leadership of the church, we embarked on a period of tremendous growth in our little Little Brown Church. We quickly grew from about 30 people in attendance each Sunday to two services on Sunday mornings with about 300 people in attendance. To accommodate the sudden increase of our church attendance we were talking about adding a third morning worship service on Sunday mornings. At that moment of expansion in our attendance we were faced with a building that would only hold about 150 people with people being stuffed in overflow rooms and isle-ways that the zoning commission in our area would have frowned upon had they known what we were doing. At that very same time a sister Christian Church congregation about ten minutes away from where we were located was experiencing a very different condition in the life of their congregation. The Central Christian Church located in the city of Van Nuys had a beautiful church building with a sanctuary that seated about 650 people. They were having only about 30 people in attendance each Sunday morning and most of them were quite elderly. Most of our people were young and they had a large number of young children as well. Both of these congregations began talking to one another about a proposed merger of the two faith communities. Each congregation possessed much of what the other congregation desperately needed. One congregation had many people but had very limited space for the people to meet in and the other congregation possessed a wonderful gymnasium, numerous rooms for both adult and children's meetings, a huge kitchen with several commercial-size stoves and refrigerators and, most of all, it had a beautiful large sanctuary for worship that would provide ample opportunity for continued numerical growth. What they lacked were people. We had the people and they had the space. It seemed to most of the people in both congregations to be a marriage made in heaven. After several church dinners together with both congregations enjoying each others' cooking and numerous opportunities to meet together for discussions and combined worship, we decided to merge our two church families into one. So, on January 9th, 1988 several hundred members of our two congregations met across the street in the church parking lot in the Van Nuys location for prayer. Following our prayer moment we all walked across the street singing with one joyous voice the words of the old hymn: "What a fellowship, what a joy divine, leaning on the everlasting arms." We had started on one side of the street as two church families but when we walked into the church sanctuary on the other side of the street we walked into the building as one, united church family. The trumpets were waiting inside the sacred auditorium ready to support our combined singing. There wasn't a dry eye anywhere. The elderly people and the young people hugged one another and the little children shouted and jumped for joy. The church officers from one congregation joined the church officers from the other congregation to form one united ruling body in the new church. Every effort was made to honor the differing points of view that we knew existed in both congregations until, in time, we knew we would all be speaking to one another with one voice and with one spirit. We still did not know what we would call this new church we had formed. Everyone was urged to put a name for the new church in a large box and in a month we would vote and let the new church decide for itself what their new name would be. Over a hundred names were submitted. We voted in three stages, gradually reducing the number of proposed names to just six names. A date was announced for the final vote and the name for the new church would be announced. From that day forward this wonderful congregation would be called: "The Church of the Valley" or, as everyone came to refer to it simply as: C.O.V. Both church facilities would be retained and used for various church functions. The Little Brown Church facility would continue with its open door for prayer 24 hours a day and would continue to be the site where many weddings would be performed in its quaint chapel as it had done for almost 40 years. The larger site in Van Nuys would be used for Sunday and mid-week worship and study services and for other larger gatherings that would be required for our growing congregation. Shortly after we had acquired our new name our oldest child, Lance, whispered in my ear one day these words: "Dad, I have never told anyone else this secret before but I was the one who submitted that name for our new church." I was so surprised and proud to hear these words from him. I have never told anyone, until now, this special secret Lance shared with me that day. It is something very special the two of us have privately shared together for more than 34 years.

17

My final steps toward receiving my doctorate

For the several years I had been pursuing my Ph.D. degree at the University of Southern California we could only afford to pay for the tuition for two enrolled classes at a time so I had to enroll in 16 semesters of instruction to complete my residence work for my degree. That amounted to eight years in all to complete my degree program. Most students begin researching and writing their required dissertation following the completion of their entire body of classwork and taking their four-day comprehensive written examination over all their studies. I, however, began researching and writing my dissertation three years earlier before I actually finished my classwork in order to save some time in completing my degree. The university had never heard of that being done like that before but they allowed me to do it with the warning that they did not believe it was a smart decision on my part as the added strain of doing this stressful research could be very bad for my health and might imperil my finishing the educational task before me. I felt that because of my working at two full-time jobs (being the Senior Minister to a very large church and teaching more than a full load of classes at Pepperdine University) and in addition, trying to be a husband and father to five growing children, that I needed to make this time-saving decision to bring my doctoral pursuit to a close as soon as I possibly could. Nevertheless, the university said to me for the second time that they felt that this huge role-overload could be extremely bad for my health and it might just lead to the discouragement on my part and cause me to simply give up on completing my degree program. What the university did not know about me was the level of my perseverance when I started something in life that I really wanted to complete.

When a Ph.D. candidate finishes his or her coursework they are required to take a four-day written examination over all the areas of study they explored in their coursework. I had five different areas of study that I was going to be tested over. I had petitioned the university to allow me to earn a degree with not just one major area of specialization (the usual route all students followed) but to allow me to earn a double major in both sociology and philosophy of education. After writing a lengthy letter explaining why my dual professions of the ministry and being a college professor would be greatly benefitted by earning a double major in these two fields, they granted me my request. However, this would mean that my final written examination would be doubly difficult because the written examination for a double major would be twice as demanding as a single major would be. So, with all my classes finally completed I set out preparing for my final written ordeal. The preparation time would take me approximately six months to adequately finish so I thought to myself: "No more vacations or family outings for me for a long while." Bummer!

The final written examination room where the Ph.D. test was to be given was huge. Approximately 400 Ph.D. candidates would be assembled for the four-day, four-hour exam. Everything rested on the student's performance on this demanding examination. If the graduate student failed this examination their quest for a doctoral degree would be over for them . . .

forever. There were no second chances. It did not matter how many years they had been studying for their Ph.D. dream. If they failed this final exam they would have to look into another profession for their life's work.

I had heard that a person could request using a typewriter and special room in which to type their answers to the examination questions instead of writing their answers out by long-hand in that big assembly hall. There were 10 very lengthy questions given to each of these 400 students in a sealed envelope with their name written on the outside of it. Each of these questions was personally designed for that particular student taking the test and it was handed to the student on the day of the examination. Very few students had ever requested to type their answers to their exam questions because they did not want to trust their typing skills for such an important moment as that. I loved to type and I had an electric typewriter that I thought would be very helpful to me so I made this request to take my exam in another room with my typewriter. I and one other student were the only ones granted that request. So, four evenings of grueling writing were set aside for these 400 hopeful students. It was a 'do or die' moment for us 400 test-takers. We were reminded by the proctors of the examination what we already knew ahead of time: "Fail this exam and your Ph.D. aspirations will be over." The Proctor in the front of the room finally said to us all: "Open your envelope and begin writing your answers!" Just before I left the room to begin typing my answers in the room next to the auditorium, a student about ten feet away from me jumped to his feet after opening his envelope and reading his ten questions, he shouted loud enough for all of us to hear: "Oh damn! I'm screwed!" He slammed his opened envelope with his exam questions down on the little desk where he had been sitting and ran out of the room. He was apparently on his way to tell his family that his educational dream had just gone up in flames. Those of us sitting near him were stunned by his actions and hoped we wouldn't have to make that very same speech to our families as well.

The typewriter I had decided to use in writing my answers proved to be a very wise choice on my part because I was finished with my 10 very lengthy questions in two hours, not four hours. I called some of my friends later on in the evening and they were all still writing their answers to their exams. We went through the very same writing exercise on the following three evenings. I was through much sooner than my other friends each time we took our written test.

Thank you, my wonderful Smith-Corona typewriter!

We were told that in three weeks each one of us would be required to return to our particular division in the university where we had done our schooling to receive our results in person from the combined gathering of all of our professors there. It was crunch time for all of us. As I previously mentioned, there were five areas in all on which all of the students were examined. Each of the areas was given a numerical grade from one to five, with five being the highest grade one could receive in each area. In order to pass the doctoral examination each student had to receive a total of 15 points over the five areas. That would amount to an average of a score of three in each of the five areas for a total of 15 points. For instance, a student could receive a score of two in one area but then he would have to receive a four in another area to average a score of three overall in each of the five areas in order to pass. So, that is what each student hoped for: an average of three in each of the five areas to pass with 15 points overall. That is all anyone wanted to do when all was said and done and that was simply to just pass the exam any way one could!

On the appointed day when the results were to be revealed, I showed up in the large waiting room of our division at the university. There were about 60 students waiting in that large room to get their results revealed to them. No one was speaking to each other. It felt like a funeral parlor. We watched each one as they were called into the inner room where all of the professors were located to announce their judgment of that particular student's performance on their final exam. Some were in there longer than others but we were all very concerned at reading their facial expressions as they left the room with the professors. Some left, crying. Some were simply very grim. Some, of course, were elated beyond description, practically hopping and skipping through the waiting room and out the door to the outside, where they could shout to the high heavens that, thank God, they had passed! Gradually, the room began to empty and the 60 graduate students were finally reduced to only one student sitting alone . . . me. It seemed as if I had been there for hours and I simply could not understand why I was the very last one to be called. I could only think of ominous reasons when, finally, my name was called to enter. My heart was pounding so very hard as I entered this inner sanctum of fateful revelations. I had worked so hard for so long and I just didn't know what I would do or what I could possibly say to Virginia and the children if I didn't receive good news on the other side of that door I was entering. "Have a seat, Mr. Keene", Dr. Bennett said to me. I noticed Dr. Audrey Schwartz, the Chairperson of my doctoral committee, sitting at the very head of the table around which 20 other professors also sat. Dr. Bennett stood up and began to speak: "The reason we have kept you, Larry, to be the final student to get their results is a very special one. As you know, each student must receive a cumulative score of 15 points over the five areas of the examination. Every once in a while a student receives a score of 'five' in an area of testing but that is very rare because a score of five is so superlative that we do not often give a grade of five out to a student. It is more than rare for a student to have ever received two fives over the five areas on their final examination. And, we have <u>never</u> heard of anyone receiving three fives on their final examination. But you, Larry, received all fives over the five areas of your examination for a perfect score of 25 for your overall total. In the entire history of our school we have never witnessed this ever happening before. This is why we have asked Dr. Schwartz to sit at the head of the table to congratulate you on behalf of our entire teaching staff and to tell you how impressed we all are with your performance on this rigorous exam." I felt like I was going to faint. I was so moved within me at this wonderful news. Before I could say a word, Dr. Schwartz was on her feet taking me in her arms and giving me a great big hug. I could feel that her cheeks were all wet as were mine as well. Everyone was applauding and sending out "atta boys" all around with various other words of support and congratulations. What a moment that was! So many tests had been taken and papers written and graded over those extended years of schooling. So many trips had been made to the university in an old car that ran on prayers as well as gasoline on those perilous trips to the school over the many years. I was so happy with what had just transpired in that room. It was almost as much fun for me as it was being introduced to the <u>Dick and Jane</u> reader in the first grade by Mrs. Fant in that little one-room school house so many years ago on the farm!

Shortly after taking and passing my grueling comprehensive examination at the university I turned in the 346-page copy of my research dissertation to my university advisors. As I said earlier, most of my graduate student friends began their research and writing of their doctoral dissertations <u>immediately following</u> the taking and passing of their demanding comprehensive examination. I had begun researching and writing my dissertation three years earlier when I was taking my coursework for my doctorate. So, by the time I had finished my coursework and had taken my comprehensive examination I was all done with everything, including my written dissertation. My research document was turned in and approved and I was finally finished. College work for me was now over!

I decided, immediately, to write a 33-page paper which was essentially a partial summary of my three-year research project of an experimental elementary school in Southern California. The paper took a careful look at the positive and negative results of racially desegregating an elementary school under very controlled conditions where the number of black and white middle-class students and the number of black and white middle-class teachers would always remain the same in that little elementary school over time. When a black student moved away from the school he or she was replaced by another black student. The same would take place when a white student would move away. He or she was replaced with a white student. The same policy applied to the black and white teachers as well. I had made millions of statistical cross-tabulations comparing the responses the students made to the written questionnaires given them over a three-year time period and I was overjoyed that the Los Angeles Unified School District had used my data extensively in constructing their own desegregation program. So, I submitted my research paper to the Harvard Educational Review, the most prestigious educational journal in the entire United States (and perhaps the world) and they sent me a letter stating that they had accepted it for publication!

They asked me, however, if I would change the way I presented my statistical data and I explained to them that I would not be willing to do that as it would take a couple of months more of very hard work on my part to rewrite that part of my paper. I explained to Audrey Schwartz, the chairperson of my dissertation committee, what I had said to the Harvard scholars and she was stunned at what I had done. She said to me: "Larry, I have been publishing my scholarly research for 30 years in various educational journals around our country and I have never been accepted for inclusion by the Harvard Educational Review. You have accomplished this feat in your very first attempt at doing so. I don't understand why you turned down their offer." I said to her: "I have been working at two full-time jobs for the past three years while going to graduate school, teaching extra classes at school for more money to support my family, and researching for years on this exhaustive project of mine. I am just tired and worn to the very bone. I simply do not have two more months of extra energy in me. I need to get back to my family again!"

18

Building our unique valley church

After receiving my Ph.D. degree from the University of Southern California, I turned my entire efforts to building and expanding the ministry of our wonderful church. One of the most meaningful experiences I had with our new church was because of a funeral I was asked to conduct on our other campus, the Little Brown Church in the Valley. One of my dear friends, Jane Beuth, came to me and told me her mother had just died and would I officiate at the funeral for her mom. Of course I was happy to do that and following the funeral I met her fiancé, Brian, who was a rabbi. I had never before had a close relationship with a rabbi so I did not know what would come from this introduction to one. Brian and my relationship really clicked. We became fast friends and spent hours and hours talking about our own separate faith journeys. What we discovered was that our viewpoints on so many theological topics were very similar. I invited him to lead several study groups at our church, mostly on subjects related to the Old Testament and his Jewish faith. When I would go on vacation, I began asking him to fill in for me on Sundays to preach to the congregation. The people loved him! He did this on several occasions and when our people knew I had to be away from the church on Sundays they would always say to me: "Get Rabbi Mayer to preach for you!" Brian has become my very best friend in life. Even though he and his family have moved to Portland, Oregon we still talk to one another for hours several days during the week. I love this man more dearly than any other man I have ever known!

As I had now finished my challenging work for my degree at the university, I poured myself into building our church into a powerful witness for Christ in the San Fernando Valley. I tried to employ the kind of thinking 'outside the box' that characterized my time in my seminary training much earlier in my life. We introduced several very original and progressive kinds of programs at the Church of the Valley that were not generally employed in any of the other Christian Churches in Southern California or, for that matter, anywhere else in the country. We encouraged women to assume places of leadership in the church, places where only men previously had held. We encouraged people from various racial backgrounds to do the same. We allowed homosexual people to gain membership in the church as well and to assume the same leadership positions that anyone else who was qualified might hold in the church. We even hired some of these individuals to be a part of our paid leadership staff in the church. It was so exciting to sit around our staff-meeting table each week with men, women, and gay staff members all sharing their perspectives and ideas on the ministry and how we, as a congregation, could do our very best in meeting the spiritual needs of ALL of our members not only the needs of SOME of them. We tried to employ a wide variety of church music within our worship services that included: gospel, jazz, old-fashioned hymns, contemporary music, and even Latin music as well. Liturgical programs celebrating the religious seasons of the year were also a significant part of our church life and were often augmented by dramaturgical presentations to give emphasis to the gospel's beauty and meaning. Sometimes we would also employ more formal clerical dress in our worship services and at other times we would dress more informally. Innovative evening services that would encourage feed-back opportunities for our congregants were also performed to keep the worship experiences for our church membership vital and contemporary intellectually, emotionally, and spiritually.

During the morning worship service, at the time of the Pastoral Prayer, the minister would move from the pulpit to the front of the congregation and kneel at a special altar that had been constructed and placed there for communal prayer. He would kneel before the people (an unusual practice in most Protestant churches) and he would invite those who wished to join with him in kneeling at the bench or around it, to come forward from their places in the congregation and join him, kneeling. Often as many as a hundred people did so. It was the highlight of our morning worship hour to be sure.

Of special interest to our church family was when we would conduct our annual "Walk Through the Bible" weekend series where a famous biblical scholar from somewhere in the world would be invited to our church as a guest to give a series of lectures or presentations for our spiritual and intellectual edification. Hundreds of ministers and members from other congregations would also attend these exciting biblical series over the years.

We also trained 52 lay leaders from our congregation to lead each Sunday's worship service throughout the year instead of having the hired staff do this spiritual task every week. This was done not to limit the role of the paid clergy in our congregation as much as it was to expand the role of the lay people in our church. We did not intend to de-sanctify the clergy class as much as to sanctify all of our laity to live up to their holy ministerial calling as Christians. In this way the spiritual maturity of our membership was developed and enriched over time. Many of these lay-leaders later enrolled in seminary because of their opportunity to lead in this way and eventually some of them became ordained ministers. Many of these lay leaders are now ministering successfully to churches throughout Southern California today. One of them is now the Senior Minister of The Church of the Valley itself, the very place that gave birth to his own ministerial ambitions and desires long ago!

Our community service on behalf of others was also an important part of our church's focus.

Monthly we would gather enormous amounts of building materials with hundreds of our church members and their friends and we would travel to Mexico to build dozens of homes throughout the years to donate to the poor people in that country. At the end of the day of our laboring on site to bring a large one-room home to reality, our job would be finished, fully constructed, fully painted, with running water and working electricity. These new occupants of the newly-constructed home always joined us during the day of working to make their dream of a new home for them a reality. The last act of the day for us workers was for us to give them the keys to their new home. And, then for all of us, it was our turn to jump into our cars and trucks to drive north to our own homes in Southern California four hours away. We were all very weary but we were quite joyous in our hearts to see the happiness in the eyes of those who had just put their little brass key into the door of their new home for the very first time realizing that they would be sleeping that night in a house that was theirs and theirs alone! In the past 30 years over 300 homes have been built by our congregation and given to poor people in Mexico.

Weekly, we would also conduct an AIDs support group on Thursday evenings. We did this for over 20 years. We fed these AIDs-infected guests of ours dinner each week and about 30 people (with members of their own families invited as well) would gather together after dinner to discuss and share together their frightful experiences of living with the deadly AIDs virus and, sadly, often sharing with their dying from this terrible disease as well. More than just dealing with the crippling physical effects of the disease of AIDs we had to help these frightened people to also come to grips with the crippling social effects of their being rejected by others, even sometimes by their own families. The anti-AIDs medicines available in those early days of the virus were very primitive by today's standards so the healing effect of our congregation's love and acceptance of these infected men and women brought tremendous hope and a sense of spiritual and physical renewal for thousands of people in the two decades of the group's important existence.

So many of our families in the church had both parents working outside the home. We increasingly felt the need to provide care and learning for their pre-school children while they were away from their children – learning which provided more than just baby-sitting for their children. After considerable planning and fund-raising on our part we opened a learning-based day care center with a director and several licensed teachers to teach and to care for those children. The program has now been running for 25 years and is widely admired as one of the most creative and successful preschool programs in Southern California.

Every month, for many many years, a large group of our parishioners would assemble on Sunday evenings at the church with numerous dishes of homemade food to take to the homeless centers around Southern California. We would serve our homeless guests their Sunday evening meal and then sit down and eat and visit with them as well. The gathering would last until late in the evening providing a terrific opportunity for the members of our church to gain a more sensitive understanding of those wonderful, often left-behind people. It helped us all to 'see', 'feel', and 'understand' more clearly who these invisible people actually were. People who were made more invisible by our inattention and neglect.

Perhaps one of the most innovative aspects of our church life was the way we chose to organize and administer the three different congregations located on our church campus. Each one of these three congregations spoke a different language: English, Korean, and Spanish. In all other church locations where English-speaking churches would 'nest' other congregations on their campus property, they would charge these foreign-speaking congregations a monetary fee and would schedule a time and place for them to conduct their own private religious service(s) on the church property of the English-speaking congregation. There would, usually, be little or no fellowship between the English-speaking members and the foreign-speaking membership on those various church campuses. It was, primarily, only a financial arrangement that the English-speaking congregation would make with the 'renting' congregation. We chose not to do things in our church that way. Our three congregations would, of course, continue to worship within the location of their own language group because of the obvious linguistic and cultural differences between them. However, we planned merged meetings between all three groups three or four times a year with shared music and short speeches with translators to communicate to the entire assembly. We would also have annual picnics together and other specially scheduled events to foster a closeness between the three congregations who shared the same beautiful campus. However, the most important part of our shared life together was in the governance of our three programs. Each congregation selected a couple of their own members to sit on a combined Official Board of the three congregations. ALL of the combined financial offerings that were collected on Sundays were collected on Monday mornings and put into a common treasury and all the bills and salaries for all three congregations were paid for from that common treasury. In this way one congregation did not come to act or feel superior or inferior to the other two congregations and, as well, all member-representatives from each congregation would share in the discussions at the Official Board meetings on matters relating to the life of each church. It was an amazing style of church governance that I had never witnessed anywhere else in the country. We would say to others when they asked us about our unusual church arrangement: "We are actually just one church which happens to be characterized by three spoken languages."

With all of this vitality being experienced within our church it was not surprising that we soon became the largest Christian Church (Disciples of Christ) west of the Mississippi River. We had more baptisms than most of the churches in America, performed more marriages in our church buildings than any church in America, and sent more people into the ministry than most other congregations in our country.

When Virginia and I retired from our beloved congregation the church collected over $100,000 to give to a scholarship fund in my name at Pepperdine University where I had taught sociology and anthropology for over 40 years. This fund would provide financial help for needy students who would be majoring in the discipline of sociology, the area of my academic expertise. Dozens of students have been able to complete their education because of this much-needed scholarship help that was made available to them through our church's scholarship fund that was established in my name. In the 86-year history of Pepperdine they had never had a church do such a tremendously thoughtful thing for the students at the university. I am so thankful to God for the generosity of our church family that invested in the good work of the school where I wore my other occupational 'hat' for so many years. That $100,000 endowment fund has grown and continues to do its generous supportive work even to this day!

Fifteen years after we moved from our location at the Little Brown Church, Virginia and I retired from our ministry with the Church of the Valley. Working as a full-time professor at

Pepperdine University for those many years while at the same time filling the role of full-time minister at our large Christian Church was a pretty heavy load for someone who had just approached retirement age. So, I happily turned over both my school job and my church job to younger people who could bring youthful vigor and vision to both tasks. Upon reflection, my 68 years in the Christian ministry and my 42 years of academic instruction as a university professor have been deeply rewarding ones for me. I could never have achieved the levels of excellence in both of these career areas of my life without my wonderful wife, Virginia, being at my side. Being the daughter of a very successful minister, she contributed invaluable insight on so many occasions about the appropriate role a minister should follow in leading a congregation of faithful followers. She also participated with me in many helpful ways at the university as well, especially in those few years when I was vice-president charged with raising funds for student scholarships. Her considerable social skills were extremely helpful to me in our raising millions of dollars for student aid. Virginia is smart, profoundly caring, and untiring in her devotion to God. Her beautiful singing voice and general musical talent raised the beauty and quality of the music we produced in each of the congregations to which we ministered throughout our many years of service. She was often asked to sing at important university functions as well. In addition to being the major force in the successful raising of our five wonderful children, Virginia also managed to record three beautiful long-play recordings of sacred music showcasing her beautiful coloratura soprano voice. The quality of the music at our church under her wise guidance, was the envy of all the churches in our denomination. At our farewell program where the sanctuary was filled with almost 700 people, the Rev. Robert Bock, our dear life-long friend, said these words about Virginia and me: "Larry and Virginia are the very best ministerial team I have ever encountered in the fifty years I have spent in the Christian ministry." It was a very touching remark and Virginia and I were deeply humbled at hearing it. Thank you, Bob!

19

Finally, finding my ultimate home and then some.

This story of mine began several chapters ago with a young child being removed from his home by the circumstances of a great world war. My first trip away from home was to an orphanage with my three sisters and then after several months at the orphanage I moved away once more, this time with my youngest sister Judy, to a foster-home in rural Washington state where I lived for three years until World War II ended.

When I left my Seattle residence as a very young child I felt a great longing and searching within me for a place of permanence and meaning in my life, a home if you will, for my increasingly restless soul. Home, initially for me, was a place. A place called Seattle with its warm concrete streets in the summer whose oozing tar-filled cracks we children played in with joy and abandon. Home was not only a warm and secure place but it was also a place that included those memorable things I greatly treasured like my used and badly worn red tricycle that was the most prized possession this five-year-old child could ever have wished to have owned. But, most of all, home for me were my mother and father and my two sisters from whom I had become separated for three long war years. What I discovered after returning three years later to a brand new home and to my parents and to my two other sisters was that long after my return from this hurtful separation there was something still very lost deep within me which needed to be found and replaced. I have come to realize over time that I am still in some ways searching for that happy and stable home which had vaporized from me many years earlier. Every separation in my later life from other significant others around me or any movement away from certain comfort zones in my life have seemed to increase this longing within me for a greater sense of security and permanence in my life. So in some important, emotional way I have learned that life for me has been a kind of continual searching for an emotional 'home' and stable environment that I could claim for my own which would provide for me some recovery or healing from my earliest feelings of abandonment.

I have found, without a doubt, the greatest part of this enduring stability and happiness through the selection of my life's partner, Virginia. On several occasions I have stated publicly that falling in love with and marrying Virginia Anderson was the smartest and most satisfying accomplishment I have ever experienced in my life. Together, we have given birth to five children who, in turn, have shared with us their five wonderful spouses. Our children have had fourteen grandchildren and many of these grandchildren have gotten married and have had children too (six grandchildren in all for us). Our large family, and their tremendous capacity for expressing unconditional love to everyone around them, have been a healing force within me and have given me a deep and satisfying feeling that my life-long search for that soul-filling 'home' I have long searched for, has finally been found.

Much of the stability and happiness I have longed for has also been achieved by me through the two career choices I have made in my life. Choosing to become a clergyman as my primary vocational pursuit has given me the opportunity to render assistance to others who have gone through similar moments of difficulty in their lives as I have. I have learned that those painful moments I once experienced in my own childhood and youth have given considerable clarity and meaning to the counseling I have been able to offer others in the course of my ministry. I have learned that the qualities of empathy and sympathy, qualities so necessary and important to someone who wants to be a Christian minister, can be better shared with those in pain and duress when that person has, himself or herself, also experienced similar pain and duress in his or her own life. I have learned that whatever we give away in life we also become filled with. So, in providing comfort and blessing to others, I in turn have become greatly comforted and blessed myself by doing so.

Secondly, becoming a university professor in sociology and anthropology has greatly appeared to the intellectual and scholarly side of my nature and to the desire within me to explore those curious boundaries of my mind. Both the spiritual and scientific approaches to learning that the Christian ministry and my university teaching have provided me have given me two very different and unique windows into the world of the 'unknown' in my life. I could not imagine navigating my life forward without the amazing contributions these two special windows into our often mysterious world have given me. The ministry has increased the capacity of my heart and soul to realize that not all things in life can be quantified or understood by what can be seen, touched or experienced by our physical senses. Through my ministerial endeavors I have come to appreciate how so much of life is non-material in nature and is real in a very spiritual, emotional, or mystical way. The scientific and rational side of me, on the other hand, has helped me to appreciate the value of carefully observing my environment and drawing helpful conclusions that can only be achieved by employing the tools of science and reason. These two very special approaches to a fuller understanding of life have helped me to find a very satisfying home to both my restless, searching soul and mind. My spiritual heart has made my scientific mind more compassionate toward others and my rational mind has given so much helpful enlightenment to my spiritual heart's more mystical understanding of things. I think I have indeed been blessed by both of these very different worlds of inquiry in my own personal home-bound quest in my life.

While the nuclear family that has enriched me these past 66 years continues to do so. My birth-family, however, is now gone. My mother, father, and three sisters have all passed away. My mother had smoked two packages of cigarettes a day for 50 years. We tried to get her to stop that terrible habit but the addiction to tobacco was too great for her to overcome. The doctor told me that her smoking shortened her life greatly. She was just 62 years old when she passed away!

My father was a smoker as well for the last 62 years of his life. His long-term smoking habit (three packages of cigarettes a day) contributed to his having open-heart surgery in the last few years of his life. His hardened and greatly clogged arteries (due to his diet and tobacco intake) made his movements around the house very difficult. He seldom went outside or to other places of amusement in the final few years of his life. Dad was only 74 when he died.

My oldest sister, Marlene, inherited mother's Polycystic Kidney ailment and in the last few years of her life she went weekly to a special clinic where all her blood was filtered and cleansed during a several-hour treatment process that left her very weak for several days until it was time for her to go through that cleansing ritual all over again. She was on a list to receive a replacement kidney for three or four years and she finally received one and it was quickly and successfully implanted in her body. For six months everything was going well for Marlene until she had a heart attack and died. Marlene was a smoker too and the doctor told me that with her already weakened body that her smoking contributed greatly to her shortened life even with the new kidney she was given. She passed away at the same age as dad did, at 74.

Roberta was a heavy smoker as well. She had a stroke at the age of 60 and lost almost all her communication with the outside world. Even though she was lovingly cared for in her last 20 years in the home of her wonderful daughter, Valerie, she was only able to communicate in one or two-word sentences. She was never able to start a sentence with anyone else on her own but was only able to respond to the sentences or questions others would ask of her. One would have to ask her probing questions to find out what she was thinking or wanting . . . questions that could be easily answered 'yes' or 'no'. She had a most pleasant and caring personality but was totally imprisoned for those last 20 years in her own world of verbal isolation. She lived longer than her parents or sisters. She finally died at 80 years of age.

Judy, the youngest of all the children, died just a few years before Roberta did. She worked very hard as the owner of a very successful restaurant in the little town of Lompoc, California. Approximately fifteen years ago she discovered that she had cancerous tumors all over inside her body and that there was nothing doctors could do to bring about any healing for her. Sadly, she passed away very quickly. As with all the other members of the family she also smoked quite heavily and the doctor said that a big part of the blame for her quick demise was the smoking habit she had since she was a young girl. Judy was only 71 when she passed away.

71 years ago my mother took me into the bathroom and forced me to smoke a cigarette that she had laced with a rubber band and a hair from a dog. I told her that I had never smoked and hated the smell of cigarettes and would never take up that filthy habit. She told me that she wished she had never started smoking herself and that she was going to ensure that I never would

follow in her steps by doing so myself, so she insisted that I start smoking the doctored cigarette she had prepared for me. It was my mother's form of aversion therapy. It worked! I never ever took another puff from a cigarette again. I think that she actually extended my life by putting me through that awful ordeal. ALL of my family's deaths were, in part, brought about by their addiction to tobacco and because of that their lives were greatly shortened. I am currently 86 years old and in good health. It is unknown how much longer my family could have all lived if they had been taken to a bathroom by someone with a doctored cigarette earlier in their lives. I am certainly glad that I was!

As I look back upon it all – my time with my family of origin and my time with my family of procreation (two wonderful anthropological terms) -- I can honestly say from the bottom of my heart that while I have been searching for a long time for a home that I felt I had once lost, I feel that today I have finally and happily found my way back to that wonderful place. "Home sweet home" were the wonderful words that someone once spoke about that glorious place. It most certainly is that to me now . . . and more!

www.ingramcontent.com/pod-product-compliance
Lightning Source LLC
Chambersburg PA
CBHW030430010526
44118CB00011B/566